PN Review 229

Volume 42, Number 5

MAY–JUNE 2016

T0164123

POEMS

FEATURES

REPORTS

REVIEWS

Editorial

Claudia Rankine's *Citizen: an American Lyric* was awarded the 2014 National Book Critics Circle Award for poetry. It had also been short-listed in the 'criticism' category. Booksellers and librarians were puzzled: where to display and shelve such a generically anomalous title? The poetry committee triumphed: Once *Citizen* was pronounced a poem, other awarding panels could follow: it received the PEN Centre USA poetry award, the Los Angeles Times Book Prize for poetry, and the NAACP Image Award for poetry. And in 2015 in Britain it received the Forward Prize for 'Best Collection'.

The word 'collection' underlines a bias in the Forward Prize's rubrics. The T. S. Eliot Prize, too, specifies 'the best collection of new verse in English'. The formulation is peculiarly English, rooted in the settled anti-Modernism that marks the editorial policies of the major established London publishers, including the one that T. S. Eliot helped to shape, promoting such works as Pound's *Cantos*, Djuna Barnes's *Nightwood* and David Jones's *The Anathemata* and famously saying, 'With most categories of books you are aiming to make as much money as possible, with poetry you are aiming to lose as little as possible.'

Citizen, partly in prose and script form, with graphic and photographic images, arranged in seven chapters, is neither a 'collection' nor 'verse'. To subtitle it a *lyric* is as provocative and, in a sense, as political as Wordsworth and Coleridge calling their 1798 collaboration *Lyrical Ballads*, which sounded like an oxymoron to contemporary readers with a settled sense of genres: the purity of the lyric was affronted to keep company with the vulgar ballad.

Rankine is by turns documentary, archival, personal, drawing in to *Citizen* the racisms she, friends and public figures have experienced, aspects of a post-colonial continuum with the experience of Black people in earlier centuries. Her use of 'lyric' relates her work to the 'lyric essay', another suggestive contradiction in terms that combines essay, memoir, verse and research, a form associated especially with women writers, and with Rankine herself, creating 'a space apart'.

One writer Rankine acknowledges as a fore-mother is Zora Neale Hurston (1891–1960), a woman closer in time and biography to the experience of enforced displacement, disempowerment and repression that slavery, followed by segregation, produced. 'Roll your eyes in ecstasy and ape his every move, but until we have placed something upon his street that is our own, we are right back where we were when they filed our iron collar off.' Hurston uses a popular idiom, elevating it to the 'literary zone' to express something larger than the individual imagination: 'Words walking without masters; walking altogether like harmony in a song.' Her language tends towards aphorism, common saws made uncommon in new contexts. 'If you kin see de light at daybreak, you don't keer if you die at dusk.' 'Ships at a distance have every man's wish on board.' 'She was too busy feeling grief to dress like grief.' Hurston heard the different speech of Georgia, Alabama, New Orleans. She entrusted her fiction to those voices, not only their testimony but their accents.

The second of Hurston's four novels, *Their Eyes Were Watching God* (1937), was written in under two months, while the author – a trained anthropologist – was in Haiti doing field work. Missing home, she conjured its voices. The book is woven of varieties of speech, the language close to the uttering body of each speaker. Harold Bloom, including *Their Eyes* in 'The Western Canon', noticed how its mimetic language belonged with the reinventions of Modernism. Hurston resisted the pressure of Black critics to be radical in prescribed ways, to contribute to 'motive fiction and social document fiction'. The inhabitants on their verandas start to talk. 'They became lords of sounds and lesser things. They passed nations through their mouths. They sat in judgment.'

In Hurston's work Alice Walker (who found and approximately marked Hurston's grave, and in 1979 edited a Hurston *Reader*) and Toni Morrison are foreshadowed. Something starts with Hurston, a women brave and resisting in the fast-flowing currents of a given literature and politics.

Of all her books, *Their Eyes* has become canonical. Clearly conceived, it touches more points in a living culture than her other work. She was, in Jean Toomer's memorial phrase, 'a genius of the South', not only an iconic figure but a considerable writer. Her book concludes with the protagonist reconciled in the most unusual and epiphanic terms: 'Here was peace. She pulled in her horizon like a great fish-net. Pulled it from around the waist of the world and draped it over her shoulder. So much of life in its meshes! She called in her soul to come and see.' The book is lyrical, it is poetic. To call it a novel is to sell it short. To call it a poem would be to sell it short, too.

'Claudia Rankine continues the way that has been opened,' Vahni Capildeo wrote in *PNR* 228. But *Citizen* is conceived and written in a different spirit from *Their Eyes*. *Citizen* needed to be generically fixed for reasons of marketing: genre as a selling tool rather than a literary identifier... Indeed the conflict surrounding the genre itself provided a marketing opportunity.

Is it time the award rules were re-drawn to protect the remnants of generic classification, tattered and frayed in the past by modernism, today by marketing? Is it time that more appropriate awards were devised for innovative work that is deliberately careless of genres? *Citizen*, described by Capildeo as 'the crystalline aggregation of "microaggressions"', is out of the ordinary and deserves to be recognised for what it is. But it is not a collection of poems. It is not a book of verse.

News & Notes

Jackie Kay

Professor Jackie Kay MBE is the new National Poet of Scotland, its Makar, succeeding Liz Lochhead. The First Minister Nicola Sturgeon made the announcement at the Scottish Poetry Library in Edinburgh where Ms Kay read one of her own poems, 'Between the Dee and the Don'. Jackie was born in Edinburgh in 1961. Her mother was Scottish, her father Nigerian. She was adopted by Helen and John Kay and brought up in Bishopbriggs, Glasgow. John Kay worked for the Communist Party and stood for Parliament; Helen Kay was the Scottish secretary of CND. Jackie's was an unusually alert home.

She read English at Stirling and her first book of poems, *The Adoption Papers* of 1991, won the Saltire Society Scottish First Book Award. Other poetry awards include in 1994 a Somerset Maugham Award for *Other Lovers*. She received an MBE in 2006.

She abandoned Glasgow for London because, she said in an interview, she grew tired of having to assert herself as a black person in Scotland. 'There is a funny thing,' she said, 'when people accept you and don't accept you. I love the country, but I don't know if the country loves me.' As a writer, she needed to understand who she was culturally, sexually, politically. 'There wasn't anybody else saying the things I wanted to say. I started out of that sense of wanting to create some image of myself.' Her poetic journey, from the staged originality of *The Adoption Papers*, can be gauged by the poem 'Pride' in the 1998 collection *Off Colour*. On a night train journey she meets, or dreams she meets, a man not unlike her natural father; she imagines a return to his village, recognising and accepting in the end her own reflection in the train window. 'There was a moment when / my whole face changed into a map.'

She lives in Manchester and is Chancellor of the University of Salford and Professor of Creative Writing at the University of Newcastle.

African Poetry Prize

The fourth Brunel University African Poetry Prize shortlist has been announced. The prize, aimed at the development, celebration and promotion of poetry from Africa, has become a prominent feature of the awards landscape. The prize, sponsored by Brunel and Commonwealth Writers, is open to African poets worldwide, who must submit ten poems for adjudication. The Chair of the judges is the energetic founder of the prize, Dr Bernardine Evaristo, Professor of Creative Writing at Brunel. Nine hundred entries were received this year; none of the ten shortlisted poets has published a first collection. The poets listed are Gbenga Adesina (Nigeria), Victoria-Anne Bulley (Ghana), Mary-Alice Daniel (Nigeria), Chekwube O. Danladi (Nigeria), Amy Lukau (Angola), Ngwatilo Mawiyoo (Kenya), Momtaza Mehri (Eritrea/Somalia), Saradha Soobrayen (Mauritius), Warsan Shire (Somalia) and Chimwemwe Undi (Zambia/Zimbabwe/Namibia). The winner will be announced in May. Previous recipients are: 2013 Warsan Shire (Somalia), 2014 Liyou Libsekal (Ethiopia), and 2015 Safia Elhillo (Sudan) & Nick Makoha (Uganda). The winners and most of the shortlisted poets of earlier years have had pamphlets published.

Asif Khan

The new director of the Scottish Poetry Library, succeeding Dr Robyn Marsack in June, will be Asif Khan. Though he grew up in Dundee and studied at Stirling University, his professional career has been in Bristol and London in 'audience engagement, business development and marketing roles covering the full breadth of the arts, from public libraries and literature to visual art and performing arts'. In 2014 he was invited by the Government of Jamaica to produce a showcase event with the new Poet Laureate, Mervyn Morris and is a trustee of The Poetry Can and sits on the board of the Bristol Poetry Institute.

Mohammed Bashir al-Aani

Middle East Eye reported on 11 March that Islamic State militants had executed the Syrian poet Mohammed Bashir al-Aani and his son Elyas. They were arrested in the eastern town of Deir Ezzor seven months ago and taken to an unknown location. Militants executed the men on charges of 'apostasy'. Aani was noted for his opposition to the government of President Bashar al-Assad and had published three volumes of lyric poetry. Aani is the most high-profile cultural figure known to have been executed by IS in Syria in 2016.

Dimitris Tsaloumas

Contributed by John Lucas

The Greek-Australian poet Dimitris Tsaloumas has died at the age of ninety-four. Born in 1921 on Leros, at that time ruled from Italy, he was involved in wartime Resistance activities, at first against Mussolini and then the German army of occupation. A chance post-war meeting with Lawrence Durrell, to whom Tsaloumas showed some poems, led to his being given a letter of introduction to George Seferis, who made encouraging noises, and as a result of this Tsaloumas published two collections, both of which he later disowned. Then, in 1952, with the Greek government making life difficult for those it considered undesirable elements, Tsaloumas, a life-long socialist, left Leros for Australia. He taught in schools in and around Melbourne, the city where he made his home, and began to publish poems in Greek. Some were translated and Thomas Shapcott, greatly impressed by these, promoted Tsaloumas's cause. In 1983 the University of Queensland Press published the dual-language *Observatory*, which won that year's National Book Council Award for

Australian Literature. As other collections followed, so recognition of Tsaloumas's worth grew, and in 1989 Con Castan published a critical study, *Dimitris Tsaloumas: Poet*. Ten years later Helen Nickas edited *Dimitris Tsaloumas: a voluntary exile, Selected Writings on his Life and Work*, and in the same year Shoestring Press published *Stoneland Harvest*, a selection of Tsaloumas's poems in English. In 2000 UQP brought out a substantial *New and Selected Poems*. Tsaloumas was by then spending each summer on Leros, where he was welcomed as a local hero. Mainland Greek poets, though, tended to ignore him, a cause of some bitterness. His last published collection, *Helen of Troy and Other Poems* (UQP 2007), is full of his characteristic blend of grand manner and earthy matter. He died, as he would have wished, on Leros.

Nida Fazli

The *Indian Express* reported the death of Nida Fazli, a popular figure at the mushairas. Ghazal singer Talat Aziz, who sang and composed many of Fazli's tunes, said, 'Here was a man who was not diluting his first impulses. He was writing as a free thinker [...] Brilliant is a small word for him. He was the last of the brilliant poets such as Ahmad Faraz and Faiz. I am also of the firm belief that he didn't get his due despite such great poetry. He deserved much more recognition than he actually got.' Fazli wasn't popular just in Urdu literature or for writing Bollywood ghazals. 'He never played to the gallery. He wrote on his own conditions and never pandered to commercial interests, poet Wasim Barelvi, Fazli's colleague and friend, insisted.

'Tadeusz Różewicz Is Dead'

Janusz Drzewucki, trans. Adam Czerniawski

Tadeusz Różewicz has died,
I thought he would never die,
but he did die this morning in Wrocław.

Tadeusz Różewicz is dead, yet the world
is there as ever, except that Tadeusz Różewicz no
longer lives in it.

Tadeusz Różewicz has died, I thought
he would never die, since he is immortal, but he
died, and yet he is immortal.

[Różewicz died on 24 April 2014]

The Poetry Archive

The Poetry Archive was formally launched as a not-for-profit organisation on 30 November 2005 at the British Library in London. This year it reaches a decade of activity and must be one of the great achievements of the poet laureateship. Sir Andrew Motion catalysed it, leaving it as an invaluable and constantly expanding legacy. During 2016 it will celebrate and be celebrated. The heroes of the enterprise are Motion and the recording producer Richard Carrington, who first met in a recording studio in 1999. Both loved to hear poets read their work and lamented that twentieth-century writers including Hardy, Housman and Lawrence were never recorded. The Archive would seek to ensure that all significant English-language poets alive today are 'properly recorded for posterity and, crucially, that their recordings are freely available to the widest audience'. In ten years they have recorded more than 350 poets. They have linked with other resource centres world-wide, 'allowing the Archive to feature increasing numbers of recordings of poets around the English-speaking world. Every week now, somewhere in the world, a poet goes into a studio to record a reading for the Archive.' And many historic recordings are now available too, including Tennyson (recorded in 1890), Eliot, Sassoon and Ginsberg.

Commenting on the changing face of recording culture, Richard Carrington said, 'How technology has moved on! In the early days, we were still editing recordings on quarter-inch magnetic tape with a razor blade. Now, the slightest extraneous detail can be edited out [...] nothing gets in the way of your enjoying each of our recordings. [...] Remembering our launch at the British Library brings back memories of our first Honorary President, [...]Seamus Heaney. [...] Now we are thrilled to have a new President, the great actor Daniel Day-Lewis, who is already proving to be another incomparable friend to the Archive [...] From the start, there have been two words that Andrew Motion and I have often used to describe the Poetry Archive. Those words are "serious" and "fun".'

Blanco Móvil

The Mexico-based international poetry magazine *Blanco Móvil* (*Moving Target*) has reached the age of thirty, with 129 issues to its credit. It has been run by a single editor, Argentine-born Eduardo Mosches. On 3 March he publicly presented a commemorative issue at a well-attended celebration. The magazine has featured poets from many of the nations of Latin America, Europe and the Middle East, and translations from the native languages. Among the poets featured are Juan Gelman, Valerio Magrelli, Verónica Volkow, Coral Bracho, Raúl Zurita, Yehuda Amichai, Pere Gimferrer and Natalia Toledo. Mosches declared, 'In its thirty years of publication, the inclusion of hundreds of poems in the magazine have constituted a single long poem, the product of a conjunction of creators in different languages [...] a long poem that survives in the memory of readers and in the print magazine.'

Title

David C. Ward wrote on the National Portrait Gallery website on 28 March

Writer Jim Harrison, who died on March 27 aged seventy-eight, reworked the legacy of William Faulkner, Ernest Hemingway, and Wallace Stegner to his own original purposes. Set in his home state of Michigan or in the Southwest, Harrison's writing charts the life cycles (and life crises) of his characters against an acute observation of the natural world and human society. His first novel, *Wolf* (1971), was a fictional memoir of a naturalist tracking wolves in Michigan. Harrison was especially successful as a writer of novellas such as *Legends of the Fall* (1979), *The Woman Lit by Fireflies* (1990), and *The Summer He Didn't Die* (2005).

Although a successful novelist, Harrison considered himself first and foremost a poet. His poetry addresses the deep sense of the spirituality inherent in nature more directly than does his prose; he was strongly influenced by Asian poetry. Harrison was also an enthusiastic cook (especially of game) and an even more enthusiastic eater; his advice for most recipes was to add more garlic.

Although Harrison lost an eye in a childhood accident, his sharp, descriptive sense of the world and the foibles of human character never dimmed. Frequently compared to Hemingway (a comparison he disparaged) because of their shared Michigan roots and interest in the outdoors, Harrison was not as 'great' or influential a writer as his predecessor. But in many senses he was the better one, not least because of his ability to write empathetically about complex people (which Hemingway could not), especially people at odds with their family and society; rare for a male American writer, he did especially well when writing about women.

He also had a sly sense of humour and of the ridiculous (again completely unlike Hemingway); his basic world-view was of a comedy, not a tragedy, although many tragic events occurred in his writings. (The influence of Asian cosmology and poetry as well as his pantheism doubtless played a part in his essentially comedic outlook.) His last several books were streaked with his humorous exasperation about the pathos of getting old. Harrison never stopped writing, even with the afflictions and pains (psychic and physical) of old age. His last book of novellas, *The Ancient Minstrel*, was published this spring.

A Letter from Robert Creeley

COLIN STILL

Film-maker Colin Still of Optic Nerve recently bought two unpublished airmail letters from Robert Creeley to the sound recordist and record producer Fred Hunter, whose 1960s Stream records released vinyl recordings of Tom Raworth, Ed Dorn, Robert Duncan, Lee Harwood, Anselm Hollo, Basil Bunting, and Stuart Montgomery. The two paragraphs below, in which Creeley proposes some reading matter & refers enthusiastically to Charles Tomlinson, are from a letter sent from Placitas, New Mexico on 8 July 1963.

```
Here's what I suggest you read, straight off, if you have
not already done so: 1) Pound's ABC OF READING, or MAKE IT
NEW--or any of his critical work directly on the base terms
of any poem, etc; 2) Fenollosa's THE CHINESE WRITTEN CHARAC-
TER AS A MEDIUM FOR POETRY--for a sense of the kinetic, in
language--which is much an American sense; 3) W.C. Williams'
AUTOBIOGRAPHY, for a sense of the American context; 4) Don-
ald Allen's THE NEW AMERICAN POETRY 1945-60, especially for
Olson's PROJECTIVE VERSE (included in the prose notes) and
for a good cross-section of the poetry which I consider par-
ticularly of the kind which now concerns you.

    I've had the good luck to have met Charles Tomlinson here
recently--and very much like and respect him--and from that
conversation I learn that the primary difficulty Englishmen
seem to have with poets as Dr Williams et al, is that they
cannot hear the line, or rather, more accurately, the partic-
ularly rhythmic structure involved. Tomlinson has taken the
trouble which I assume was not simple to listen as closely
as possible to the literal structure of the words. For ex-
ample, he's obviously absorbed Williams' structure in poems
like OF ASPHODEL et al--as his present work shows; and earlier
he had gone to school with Stevens etc. I don't see that
there's any short way round that means of learning.
```

Letter from Trinidad

On Becoming a Belmont Exotic Stylish Sailor

VAHNI CAPILDEO

Christmas brought an experimental *Macbeth* to one quarter-acre of Port of Spain. The theatre began outdoors, in the sloping driveway. A stainless steel jug sat on a wooden table that someone had painted silver long ago. Night-time: the neighbourhood security lighting glared. A check was kept on the gateway. Whoever crossed the threshold had water poured over them; flowers poured out with the water; the water poured onto the ground. 'You must be purified of your sins', the decolonised witch admonished the audience, who were then ushered through an ironically puffed perfume wall of *Burberry Brit* to change them from the oil-producing state of everyday. A hunting knife and pine bough hung from the lamp ornamented with metal flowers: Birnam Wood and the castle intertwined. A man was bound in lengths of gold tinsel to another lamp, which would be ripped from the ceiling if he moved. A cake was prepared with enough candles for everyone, briefly, to have a wish and watch their breath act upon the flame. The Banquo-banquet would be a general birthday for this line of inheritors. There was one flaw: the KingQueen could not be crowned, except in absentia. Macbeth herself had flu.

'I can't go back without *something*,' the witch wailed to the unbound victim.

'All right,' he said. His journalist hat tipped over his poet-brain.

Another night, they drove into the night.

The houses in this area had careful, smaller gates. They were graciously built and often had been extended by their owners. A certain number of killings was known to happen, especially since the recirculation of small firearms in the region, but the core of respectability survived, seasoned and old.

'Hello, goodnight...I interviewed you...You don't remember?...Yes, it would have been about...ten years ago...We were wondering if...Well...'

She tuned in and out to his voice, which was singing and testing, like a lyric being workshopped.

'We're *outside your gate*, actually,' came the competition-winning clincher cadence.

Jason Griffith did not care whether the two young people – young to him, a Gemini of 1927 vintage – were poets, journalists, a couple, or cult members. They had come to hear about Sailor Mas.

To take part in Trinidad Carnival is to be a masquerader; to 'play mas'. To be a Mas is utterly different. Certain characters incarnate the spirit of Carnival. They cannot be reduced to bikini and beads. The 'Moko Jumbie' stilt walkers, even in their name, recall the ferocious god they invoke. You pay good money to stave off the angry attentions of the 'Jab Molassie', the black-smeared molasses devil, who blows a whistle and dances restrained by a chain. I have heard two histories for this character: a freed slave using molasses as cut-price body paint; the spirit of a slave who has been put to death in boiling molasses: and find truth in both. The 'Fancy Sailor' emerged in the nineteenth century as an imitation, satirical, extravagant, of crew disembarking from war ships.

In the years since 1949, when Mr Griffith brought out his first 'sailor band', the appearance and scope of the role had grown. Surreal, multi-coloured creations of swansdown and sequins could tower more than the height again of their often six-foot-plus masqueraders, who took pride in making or customizing their own costumes. Special dance steps evolved. It became a matter of precision to dance 'drunken sailor' or 'rock the boat'. The Sailors had their secrets. Mr. Griffith's eyes flashed as he imitated gamblers newly on shore throwing dice, one of the tiny gestures from which whole sequences and postures could be elaborated. After much else, there was the unlocking of a side room. Way above head level and many times larger than our heads, there were the wire frames and the masks of Mr Griffith's playing and making. When he locked them in again, or us out, I felt them waiting.

Back in England, and determined to find ways of relating word and action that were not 'performance' – unconsciously drawn to *make mas*, I continued to seek formal movement training. Was it possible to clear the imaginary sea from my feet and be attentive to what was around me, to what I was about; no more than that? I was like a lyric poem being edited.

The community hall had a wooden floor, fire extinguishers, and a row of neutral masks, i.e. white masks. The teacher had forbidden us to read the drama theorist whose method she followed. We would make discoveries. For example, the neutral mask was not a character; however, the ones with a softer jaw and curved lips were female, 'the woman of all women', and worn by the women in our group. We worked on becoming Her, existing in the present, without learnt habits. The exercise consisted in waking up for the first time ever, and discovering oneself to have been sleeping in a cave; embodying this without speaking, and conveying it without acting... As the sleeping mind's activity is inward, and waking breaks the rhythm of breath, my Mask opened its eyes with a gasp and a tiny, all-over shudder. This was wrong. It implied a past. Characters have pasts; the Mask does not. The vestigial history of a second's transit from a sunk state to a perceptive one was too much. How, then, did the exercise work? Perhaps it was a language problem. The infinitesimal point of being awake was the beginning; not being woken, or becoming awake. I seemed stuck with percipient, sentient being; unable to wake as Neutral Mask, inoculated with resistance to it. For it recalled to me the baby-bird innocence, the waiting to be fed, of people for whom it is repeatedly the first time ever, whenever they come up against a belief on which someone inconveniently has acted.

The old Admiral had queered me from Mask. No choice remained but to become a Mas. That year, the sailors set out as 'A Touch of Nature'. As a Belmont Sailor, blistering under a hummingbird headpiece, for twenty hours over the two days before Ash Wednesday, with impunity I danced the darkest streets, the ones that make the news. Without gender, I sent up a whiff of talcum powder – mock gunpowder – towards pretty girls who dodged, or the homeless persons' shelter where a bamboo-thin man gave a thumbs up. Without a lifespan beyond or other than Carnival, I leant against cemetery walls or sat with my feet in the gutter and had lunch out of a Styrofoam box. Without identity, I was approached by husbands and fathers whose shy wives and children wanted a photo with 'a Mas'. The inhabitation of a stylised, transhistorical 'I' was indistinguishable from a 'We'.

I realised the important social function of Mas was partly like the English parish custom of 'beating the bounds'. It kept the streets open; the streets supposedly impassable, as society deteriorated. There was no need to fracture or reinvent the syntax of movement or to theorise the erasure of self. And when some of us gathered to protest the murder of a visiting musician and the Mayor of Port of Spain's apparent condemnation of women's vulgarity inviting abuse, it was no surprise to find that the pink-shirted man with the VOX POPULI, VOX DEI placard standing beside me had been a fellow Belmont Sailor. 'You remember me? I was one of the insects', he said.

Letter from Wales

Sam Adams

On 1st March, St David's Day, Literature Wales, the administrative and funding agency for literature this side of the border, announced the appointment of a new National Poet: Ifor ap Glyn. In the words of the press release, he will represent 'the best writing from Wales on the national and international stage'. From its inauguration in 2005, it was intended that a Welsh-language poet should alternate in the role with one whose work was largely, if not entirely, in English. Ifor ap Glyn has twice won the Crown at the National Eisteddfod (in 1999 and 2013) and published five volumes of poetry in Welsh. Unsurprisingly, Welsh is his first language, but he was born and brought up in Pinner, in the London borough of Harrow. Elton John and Michael Rosen were near enough neighbours and contemporaries. Therein lies an important lesson: as long as the family remains proud and firm in the Welsh language, the children will thrive in it, despite the omnipresence of English.

Traditionally, Crowned Bards, and Welsh poets in general, have risen from the ranks of teachers, academics and ministers of religion. Ifor ap Glyn, born in 1961, is from a newer mould. Since graduating from Cardiff University he has had a career in the media. He has a considerable reputation as television scriptwriter, producer and presenter. If you can call to mind a BBC 4 series called 'Pagans and Pilgrims: Britain's Holiest Places', or another programme on the same channel, 'The Toilet: an unspoken history', then you will have had an opportunity to appreciate his skill as writer and producer, and (Praise be!) an easy, undemonstrative style of presentation, which in these days of waving arms and heavy, misplaced emphases, few seem capable of. He is a founder member and creative director of *Cwmni Da* ('Good Company') a television production company based in Caernarfon, and a major creative force in Welsh-language media. He was shortlisted for the Grierson Award in 2008, for 'Frongoch: Birthplace of the IRA' and has won a BAFTA Cymru awards for the series *Popeth yn Gymraeg* ('Everything in Welsh') and *Lleisiau'r Rhyfel Mawr* ('Voices of the Great War').

The public dimension of his new role will not disconcert him. At university in his twenties he was the front man of a rock group called *Treiglad Pherffaith* ('Perfect Mutation' – make of it what you will), and 2008–2009 he was Wales' Children's Laureate. He has twice performed at the Smithsonian Folk Life Festival, Washington DC, where the Welsh language and culture are celebrated in a way London has never yet considered. In short, he is a splendid representative of the bilingual Welsh in the technological world, justifying all that is being done by activists and Welsh Language Acts to secure the continuation of the language, in the face of indifference and even hostility from within Wales and without.

Ifor ap Glyn is our fourth National Poet, having been preceded by Gwyneth Lewis (2005–2006), Gwyn Thomas (2006–2008), and Gillian Clarke (2008–2016). At the outset, it was envisaged that the role would change hands fairly frequently, but it has lodged with Gillian Clarke for the simple reason that her performance of it has been exemplary. She has been an outstanding ambassador for poetry and for Wales, here and overseas.

The beech buds are breaking. I feel so happy.
I snapped the bare twigs in a wood
A month ago. I put them in a wine bottle
Filled with water, not for the twigs, for the light
Blown bubbles to float in the shine of the water.
[...]

The floor of the wood glimmered with white bones;
Little, silver skulls eyed us darkly, and the lambs
Leapt away round the hill. The blood of birth
And life stained the pale bones of the past.
[...]

The child sleeps, and I reflect, as I breathe
His brown hair, and watch the apple they gave him
Held in his hot hands, that a tree must ache
With the sweet weight of the round rosy fruit
[...]

It was very strange to watch him sail
Away from me on the calm water,
The white sail duplicate [...]
When they returned the exhilaration
Of the familiar morning had gone. I felt
As though on the water he had found
New ways of evasion, a sheet
Of icy water to roll out between us.

I remember the excitement I felt when, in the summer of 1970, Meic Stephens, editor of the magazine, showed me the four poems a complete newcomer, Gillian Clarke, had submitted to *Poetry Wales*. There was a marked preponderance of male poets in the lists of contributors at that time, though Ruth Bidgood, Sally Roberts Jones and Alison Bielski appeared fairly regularly. The outlook has changed since. Even now, typing the above extracts from Gillian's poems, I receive an echo of that sense of discovery we experienced then. Whatever may have been happening elsewhere, or may have happened since, there was no precedent in the scores of fat envelopes addressed to the editor that prepared us for them. Here was a young woman, mother to three children, writing directly out of life, existentially if you like, about relationships, interests and concerns, including the quotidian and domestic, with acute observation, delicacy and tact, and unstrained phrase-making that excited the ear and mind. In another year she had published enough poems to make an impressive booklet, *Snow on the Mountain*, which I edited in the Triskel Poets series. Since then she has been constantly productive. There are a further fourteen books by my count, ten from Carcanet, including *Collected Poems* (1997). With all that, and more, she has given readings at venues throughout the UK, in Europe and America, and devoted much of her time to encouraging interest in poetry among young people in schools and colleges. She became the second Welsh poet (after R S Thomas) to win the Queen's Medal for Poetry in 2010 and was admitted to the Gorsedd of Bards at the National Eisteddfod in 2011.

Although her primary creative medium is English, she has long since 'crossed the bridge' to become a Welsh speaker. She occasionally writes in Welsh and employs her second-language skills in translations of both poetry and prose. In all her travels she is as enthusiastic a champion of Wales and Welsh culture as she is of poetry.

Ifor ap Glyn's first appearance in the role of National Poet will be on 31 May at the Hay Festival, when he and Gillian Clarke will share the platform.

Charles Tomlinson at Bristol

C. K. STEAD

The British poet Charles Tomlinson died on 22 August 2015 aged eighty-eight. The following is from a memoir I am intermittently writing, this extract about my time as a PhD student on a scholarship from New Zealand at the University of Bristol, 1957–59, where my supervisor was Professor L. C. Knights, and Tomlinson was a member of the English Department.

~

Another visitor to the Department was the Canadian-born, American-by-adoption, critic Hugh Kenner, already a notable Eliot scholar. I don't now remember much of his lecture but I remember his natty bow tie and mop of curly hair, and how his at first disconcerting speech (a consequence of deafness in childhood) contrasted with Lionel Knights's smoothness and fluency introducing him; and yet how the keen intelligence and originality shone through. This was the man who made me aware I needed to know more about Ezra Pound, and who gave the idea of 'Modernism' an intellectual edge – made a puzzle and a challenge of it.

One purpose of Kenner's Bristol visit was to cement his association with Charles Tomlinson, a junior lecturer in the Department, and the only British poet whose work Kenner felt was in tune with important things that were going on in American poetry. I can't now quite disengage my present overview of Kenner from the much less I would have known about him then. He is author of one of the great books of twentieth-century literary criticism, *The Pound Era* (1972) – great not only for its intelligence and scholarship but for liveliness, originality and readability. Yet Kenner can also seem at times a critic with quite extreme quirks and crankiness, prone to clever but absurd overstatement, like a brilliant drunk in full flight. But in that year he was giving Charles Tomlinson a start he might never otherwise have had, putting him in direct touch with American poets he admired, William Carlos Williams and Marianne Moore, and persuading his own American publisher, McDowell Obolensky, to take Tomlinson's collection of poems, *Seeing is Believing*, which no publisher in England (Charles said he'd tried them all) would touch.

This was the time when the British poets of the Movement, in reaction against the flamboyance of Dylan Thomas, George Barker and the 'new Apocalypse' of the 1940s, were being defined and displayed in anthologies, from which Tomlinson had been excluded. Hell hath no fury like a poet shut out of a currently fashionable anthology, and Tomlinson was busy scourging the Movement in journals on either side of the Atlantic – in *Poetry* (Chicago), and in *Essays in Criticism* (Oxford) where he devoted no fewer than nine pages to the punishment of what he called 'the Middlebrow Muse'. These reviews were followed up with the same message when he was given the chapter 'Poetry Today' to write for the distinctly Leavisite *Pelican Guide to English Literature*, Volume 7, edited by Boris Ford.

To me Tomlinson appeared as an interesting specimen of one kind of Englishness, a man whose father sometimes believed, and liked to claim, he was of Royal blood on the wrong side of the blanket, and that he had married beneath him in that his wife, the poet's mother, had been a Leicestershire mill-girl. Tomlinson senior had lost his job as foreman in a factory that made jam pots, but was expert at fishing in the canals – which must have made the Eliot lines especially redolent to the son when he first encountered them in 'The Waste Land':

While I was fishing in the dull canal
On a winter evening round behind the gashouse
Musing upon the king my brother's wreck.

As a student at Cambridge Tomlinson had not been happy until, I think in his second year, Donald Davie became his tutor. Davie, who can't have been many years older than his charge, was also a poet, alert to what was happening in the American poetry scene, a critic as readable as Kenner but less eccentric, and interested especially in the syntax of poetry which he characterised as 'articulate energy'. He and Tomlinson formed a bond that lasted a lifetime.

After graduating, and teaching unhappily in a school in Camden Town, Tomlinson scored a post as private secretary to the British writer Percy

Lubbock, then living in Italy, in Lerici; but he was dismissed after three weeks, probably, he thought, because his genteel employer found his flat Midlands 'a' vowel unacceptable. Lubbock, he said, believed even 'ants' should be pronounced 'aunts' – but he allowed Charles and his wife Brenda to stay on there in a *villino* adjoining the gardener's cottage, thus giving the Tomlinson sensibility an Italian airing from which it never looked back. It was a region the couple were to return to often.

Tomlinson was seven years my senior and, though only a junior lecturer, was my senior also in status. We were amiably aware of one another without being close, and met regularly in graduate seminars, presided over by Knights and attended by most of the English Department staff. In 1958 he and Brenda had just moved to a rural location with the wonderfully English address of Brook Cottage, Ozleworth Bottom, Wotton-under-Edge. There was no phone, and never would be one. If a phone call was necessary they climbed the hill to a payphone. Charles and Brenda had met while in their teens and were still married at his death seventy years later. The cottage was to remain their home. They would travel a great deal, but always come back to it. Their two daughters grew up there. Charles was also admired as a painter but I don't recall that I ever saw any of his work.

Many years later, at a conference in Tubingen on poetry and regionalism, he and I would reminisce warmly about the L. C. Knights days in Bristol. By that time, I noticed, the Midlands accent was pretty much gone, replaced (though perhaps not with absolute security) by what used to be called R. P. – received pronunciation – meaning 'correct'. Knights had long since moved back to Cambridge, to the King Edward VII Chair, where F. R. Leavis, his old colleague and more famous contributor to the critical journal *Scrutiny,* who would probably have liked that eminent seat for himself, referred to him as 'Professor Judas'. This Regius chair should have been the ultimate academic triumph for Knights but when I visited him there, and he walked me in Queen's College gardens, and took me to lunch in the College, it was soon apparent he was not altogether happy. To Frank Kermode, who would succeed him there, he reported his dissatisfactions and remarked, 'Oh for the road not taken!' I have no idea what this alternative road might have been.

Tomlinson stayed on in the Bristol Department his whole working life, in the end I think occupying the Winterstoke professorship, the one Knights had held in the 1950s.

But in 1957 I was (perhaps without good reason, certainly without careful consideration) put off his poetry partly just by his manner in person, a look of depleted energy, in fact of such profound, unrelenting weariness I felt that if it was not an illness then it had to be an affectation; and by something in the lines themselves – a kind of *dis*engagement, as if the words had been chosen with immense care, but with a faint feeling of distaste.

To Charles Brasch I wrote that *Seeing is Believing* was probably a good collection, certainly displaying 'a sharp visual perception driving a keen intelligence – but a little precious, a little gutless'.

~

The extract ends there. I wish I could say the effect of Tomlinson's death has been to make me recognise my error, but I have looked again at some of his poetry and find there's a difference of temperament so absolute that my mind begins to shut off when I read him. Two critics I greatly admire, American Hugh Kenner and British Donald Davie, have told me I am wrong about Tomlinson. But where Davie finds in his work 'an exquisitely accurate register of sense impressions', I run up against what seems to me a wall of abstraction and effete discourse.

These are the critical conversations poetry constantly requires those of us who are serious about it to have – and there are no right answers, no final resolutions. Here are some lines by Tomlinson which Davie strongly recommends because, he says, they 'insist upon the Otherness of the non-human world'. Perhaps they do, and readers will see what he means. They come from a poem called 'Cézanne at Aix', so I assume the mountain is Mont Sainte Victoire, which Cézanne painted so often:

And the mountain: each day
Immobile like fruit. Unlike, also
—Because irreducible, because
Neither a component of the delicious
And therefore questionable,
Nor distracted (as the sitter)
By his own pose and, therefore,
Doubly to be questioned: it is not
Posed. It is. Untaught

Readings of Two Poems by Samuel Beckett

THOMAS KINSELLA

Cascando

1

why not merely the despaired of
occasion of
wordshed

is it not better abort than be barren

the hours after you are gone are so leaden [5]
they will always start dragging too soon
the grapples clawing blindly the bed of want
bringing up the bones the old loves
sockets filled once with eyes like yours
all always is it better too soon than never [10]
the black want splashing their faces
saying again nine days never floated the loved
nor nine months
nor nine lives

2

saying again [15]
if you do not teach me I shall not learn
saying again there is a last
even of last times

last times of begging
last times of loving [20]
of knowing not knowing pretending
a last even of last times of saying
if you do not love me I shall not be loved
if I do not love you I shall not love

the chum of stale words in the heart again [25]
love love love thud of the old plunger
pestling the unalterable
whey of words
terrified again
of not loving [30]
of loving and not you
of being loved and not by you
of knowing not knowing pretending
pretending

I and all the others that will love you [35]
if they love you

3

unless they love you

[1936]

Cascando:

TITLE: pouring; shedding, as in bloodshed; vomiting.

PART 1: A tired poet urging himself to try once more.

Lines 1–3: Settling, once more, for the old tried, and abandoned, excuse for the pouring out of words...

Lines 5–14 : his tired love poem...

Line 4: thinking it better to force it and do it wrong than not to try.

Lines 5–6: Standard opening of a love poem: the beloved departed; imagery slow and leaden.

Lines 7–9: Dragging of line 6 particularised as the hauling up from the sea-bed of the skeletons of past loves, their eye-sockets open for the eyes of the beloved.

Lines 10–11: Repeat of line 4; the old loves, marked by the black sea-bed of desire. Would it not have been better for the lovers to try, even at the risk of failure...

Lines 12–14: ...and 'too soon' (though it is not their first effort), seeing again the failure of love to surface from the sea-bed – in nine days, as drowned bodies are said to do; in nine months, as in pregnancy; or in nine lives, like a cat: incantation on 'nine' as the tired poem fades.

★

PART 2: An editorial consideration of Part 1.

Line 15: The love poem, for the nth time...

Lines 16–24: ...its cliches parodied...

Lines 25–6: ...including the basic love image of the heart, seen in forceful action;

Lines 27–8: the 'stale words' trying – and failing – to settle themselves...

Lines 29–34: ...into substance and coherence.

Lines 35–6: A summary of the meaninglessness, for him, of the whole matter.

37: A tired signing off.

Saint-Lô:

Ten years later. In relationship with *Cascando*.

Line 38: 'Vire': swirling, related to the pouring of 'cascando'. The name of the river pouring in the Vire Valley through Saint-Lô. Atmosphere of liveliness; sensitivity. Still in shadow, but the shadows different from those in *Cascando*.

Line 39: Sensitivity at the point of rebirth; activity of line 38 to continue through 'bright ways' as through shadow...

Line 40: ...while the exhaustion of *Cascando*, freed of its negative presences...

Line 41: ...vanishes down into its proper world.

Saint-Lô

Vire will wind in other shadows
unborn through the
bright ways tremble
and the old mind ghost-forsaken [40]
sink into its havoc

[1946]

From the Archive

Issue 111, Sep–Oct 1996
Stephen Burt

AFTERMATH

Losing you, yes; a sleepless convalescence,
then waking next to sour metaphors;
from bed I counted shiny parking meters,
their single-file chorus by the fence -
your palace guard, or else discovered traitors,
each armoured head pinned up on his own lance.

From the Journals of R. F. Langley

The poet R. F. Langley (1938–2011) was also, privately, a prolific prose writer. Extracts from his journals, which he began in 1969, first appeared in *PN Review* in 2002, and a selected volume, *Journals*, was published by Shearsman in 2006. The notes to Carcanet's recent edition of Langley's *Complete Poems*, edited by Jeremy Noel-Tod, cite a number of unpublished journal entries that directly informed the writing of his verse.

4 June 2006

On the pool by the hide, beyond Lime Kiln Sluice, the large island is smothered in yellow flowers, low to the ground in a mat, with red runners stretching over the soil, under and between them, reaching the shore, plunging over into the water. I can only think that this is creeping cinquefoil. A common sandpiper walks and bobs amongst it, pecking. There is a heron, moving its feet cautiously, bending, a kink in its neck, stabbing with a considerable splash, catching a small silver fish crosswise in its beak most times. An egret operates in contrast. It runs in the water, lifting its yellow feet clear at each step, stabbing to right and left, picking insects off the surface as well as fish from beneath. When it stops running, it works its feet up and down in the mud below the surface, disturbing its food...

As the heron moves, it makes, of course, ripples. All ripples, of course, move away from it, they widen round it, spread out in front of it. They throw up white stripes of reflection, which slide up the bird's breast and neck, slip forward under its chin, and move steadily out along its bill, which is wet, so that there they often glint like a strung-out necklace, then vanish off the pointed tip. So it is softly massaged by glowing lines, moving over its white breast and neck, over the black pairs of dashes down its throat, out along the bill which is yellow-green as if freshly painted, without disturbing a feather.

That magic – light coming up from below. Lines that curl round its body and slide unbroken up it. The heron's hard eye, a tight yellow circle with a black centre, unblinking, seems as if frozen in awareness of the gentle caresses. Excited into immobility. Then it stabs down and the thick white spray jumps as high as its back.

28 June 2006

Back to Reydon Wood on my own for another look at the timber stacks in the clearings, where we found Thanasimus beetles. Sunny, early afternoon. Dapple at its richest. The shadow of my head, domed, hair very short, appearing in the patches of sun on the wood floor ahead of me and reminding me of other similar projections – especially one onto a sunlit column of Préty marble in Saint Philibert in Tournus, at the south corner of the building when I was standing in the aisle, about to leave, and remembering, I recall, sunlight in the kitchen in Longways, Devon, years ago, when I had been standing near the sink, behind the breakfast bar, talking to Mirrie about poetry. I must have been a schoolboy then...

I walk slowly, alone, in the wood, blinded at the transitions from clearing to under the canopy. What are the plants, then? Bramble... with some flowers... wood dock... honeysuckle... wild strawberry on the edge of the darker places, no flowers or fruit that I see, but leaves... A small willowherb again. Herb bennet in flower with hairy seed heads, and buttercups of course. The yellow pimpernel, long runners with pairs of leaves... The logs on the stacks must be ash and hornbeam, the bark still tight and intact on them, the ash matt pale grey, the hornbeam vertically striated with silvery, glossy strips, a darker grey, with orange about it...

And two more beetles, wasp beetles, Clytus arietis, again specialists on stacked timber, again, like Thanasimus, powerfully coloured, this time black and yellow, their reddish legs too long for those of a wasp, their searching a little too quick and limber. Find stacked logs, expect bright beetles.... Enchanter's Nightshade, fine detailed white flowers, suiting the strawberry and yellow pimpernel and herb bennet round the clearings, and on the edges of the stripped places. Flowers to stoop over and focus closely.

Four Poems

ANDREW WYNN OWEN

A Sign at CERN

'A Higgs,' it reads, 'makes gravity.'
Next step? All being, moving, doing spring:
    The genomes' sinuosity
Of protein: their controlled tornado-string
    And turns where ribbonings entwine
With redoublings, their
Cytosine, guanine, thymine, adenine
Stitches in the fabric. All codes we wear
Were hardwired in that atomic hardware.

    Take this rock, tied to a star,
Conglobing in its grip the massive weight
    Of mountains, makers of beaux-arts,
And all the chattering soldiers of debate
    Who tilt their heads like jays and spin
Narratives on the loss
Of energy that scatters from their skin
While altogether elsewhere comets cross
And plasma clouds congeal like candyfloss.

    Now take a dehydrated willow,
Weeping at every brand, its structure rolled
    For layer on layer – a cigarillo
Of bark and sap, mathematically-controlled
    Epiphenomenon of carbon
        Concealing up its sleeve
A blueprint of its promised re-creation:
When rain arrives, those seeds it stores will leave
And redesign a river with their weave.

    Look, Googler! Motors churn a plough
Through fields in France where battlelines were drawn
    As leaflife nods its splitness now
From world-at-war. A hurtling lapwing's borne
    On feather-licking air. Its motion
        Behaves as ever: time
Relates, connects, elides – lines of devotion
Erase division. Out of dugout's grime,
Convolvulus, dormice, thrilled tourists climb.

Thoughts in Sunshine

    It hurts, it hinders, it
        Elects to stay:
It sweeps uncertainty and fear away.

    It moves in me, I feel,
        And proves me real.
It makes resilience from my wistfulness
        When loss, its rival, starts to steal
From every scene of living. I confess
        I find, time running,
        My heartbeats answer less
To all I have been dazzled by:
Bedizened life, a thickened sky,
    This All that should be stunning.

    It sings, it singes, it
        Assails me now:
It troughs and overturns me like a plough.

    It finds me by a wall
        Where blossoms fall.
It blazes fresh assent across the day
    And cues each blade of grass to call
Its hopes to hold. Remain! It opts to stay
        And flashes slightly
        As I retrace my way
(But faster, energised, on fire
With lift, elation, new desire)
    And smile again, more lightly.

The Door

Distracting rays were shining round my door
      And so I stood
    And stepped across the landing floor
    To see if any light-source could
Be ascertained but, once I was outside,
      I checked my stride.

Out there I found a stretching corridor,
      Down which I walked.
    I had not noticed it before.
    On every lintel, names were chalked
And soon I stalled at one, to me well-known:
      It was my own.

The hinges creaked. I cautiously went in,
      Enjoying there
    A room where sunlight lapped my skin
    And central was a swivel chair.
It spun about. I felt a smile extend:
      'Good morning, friend.'

This figure gestured me towards an arch
      Marked 'Happiness'
    And I, determined, moved to march
    Its way, but paused: 'I should express
Some thanks—' my friend, however, waved and said,
      'You go ahead.'

Once I had ventured in I felt betrayed,
      As I discerned
    A maze of winding walls that made
    Me dizzy, sad, until I turned
One corner and (in hope of what?) I saw
      Another door.

Eager, I entered, to a gallery
      Closely comprised
    Of portals, each a vacancy
    For liberty. I realised
I'd never loved a room. It is the door
      That I adore.

Ramblers

'What silver-wheeled machinery, beyond—'
    I lose it as I think.
I goggled noonlong in a muddy pond
      And, though I blink
Away now, frantic scamperings of frogs
Still flash by, wiring, scintillant as drugs.

'What beauty been—' a friend began, and stopped to sing
    Breathtakingly. Irradiance encased
      Tree stump, loose foliage, a line
    Of poplars. Sunlight flared. I felt displaced
      And swathed in what? A wine.
A window. Disconnect. You could say anything.

    'A metal caterpillar riding high
On fortune's wheel.' 'Or no, a grounded shooting star
      Still billiarding through countryside
    From when it fell here first, when summer sky
      Was thick with suns.' 'Let slide:
It was a train.' So there we were. Now here we are.

Encounters with Bashō

Emily Grosholz

If you fly into Tokyo, and then drive along its freeways to a downtown hotel, and then stare from your hotel room on the top floor out at the serried skyscrapers shimmering against the night sky, you might well misunderstand the city. Behind the towers and apartment buildings and crowded houses, there is a square myriad of green spaces hidden away, but you must set out on foot to discover them. If you walk around behind, for example, the lovely Rihga Royal Hotel, you find Okuma Garden next to Waseda University, created by Shigenobu Okuma, who also founded the university in 1882. His statue looks out over the lawn, the lotus-covered pond, and the paths studded with small stone pagodas and lanterns. Skirting the edge of the hotel and heading west along Shin-Mejiro Street, noting the old-fashioned street cars, you should keep an eye out for errant bicyclists, who don't really obey the traffic rules though, laden with groceries or small children, seem to be having a good time. In two blocks, if you look carefully to the left past well-disguised entrances, you come to the threefold pond and tree-crowded hill of the garden Kansen-En, so beautiful in early winter that it brought tears to my eyes. Situated next to the Shinto Misu Inari Shrine, whose origins lie a thousand years in the past, the garden was created in 1774 for the Tokugawa Shogunate, which ruled Japan from 1603–1868 and defined the Edo Period. The city of Tokyo, which now encircles thirty million inhabitants, began as the small fishing village of Edo around 1450; in 1721, it was the largest city in the world, with one million inhabitants, but it has been regularly devastated by fire, earthquake and war throughout its history.

Tokyo lies between the great Tamagawa ('gawa' means river) to the west and the Aragawa and the Edogawa to the east, which flow from the hills behind the city into Tokyo Bay, but the whole area was originally a marsh and is threaded by small rivers. During preparations for the 1964 Olympics, Tokyo instituted the dubious strategy of suppressing many of these streams, covering them with streets or concrete channels and turning them into underground sewers in order to modernise the waste disposal system. (In the area around Shibuya, the neighbourhood that will be the hub of the 2020 Olympics, for example, the Shibuyagawa Renaissance Group is trying to reclaim part of the area where the Onden and Uda streams flowed into the river that carved out the little valley, and to plant new trees along its banks.) So if you continue on past Kansen-En, and turn right across Shin-Mejiro Street, you cross a plum tree-lined channel, which marks the suppression of the Kandagawa. On the day I walked along it, the flow was substantial and gave it the charm of a mid-Paris canal, enlivened by the music of flowing water and the cries of birds: great squawks from the enormous black crows and songs from the smaller warblers.

Heading back east, I skirted the Shin-Edogawa Park, and came to the Bashō-An, a small shrine that marks the house of the poet Bashō (1644–1694) on a steep slope dominated by a great gingko tree that was shedding its golden fans all over the stone steps up to the ultra-modern St Maria Cathedral at the crest of the hill, on Mejiro Street. Bashō set forth on a spring morning in 1689 on a nine-month trek through the hills and dales north of Tokyo, to the west coast on the Sea of Japan, then inland towards Lake Biwa near Kyoto, and recorded his journey in the *Oku-No-Hosomichi* (*Narrow Road to a Distant Province*). His health was already in decline, and though he lived long enough to record the trip in prose and poems, he died a few years afterwards. So the book begins: 'The moon and the sun, months and days / Are transient figures for countless generations, / and the years that come and go are wanderers too.'

The train and subway systems in Tokyo are a marvel of engineering, but present a rather daunting complexity when you first arrive: there are so many lines and so many stations! However, once you sort it out it makes sense, and all the station names are transliterated into Roman letters. Shinjuku Station is a major hub: from there you can head west on the Seibu Shinjuku line to Kami-Igusa Station, and walk to the Chihiro Art Museum in about ten minutes, past a small tree farm. The museum houses the works of picture-book artist Chihiro Iwasaki (1918–1974); Japanese people of my generation grew up with her books and are well aware of the passion that drove her work. (There is a second museum devoted to her work in the north, in the Prefecture of Nagano, near the snow-covered Hida Mountains.) She used her skills as a calligrapher and water colourist to bring joy back to Japanese children after the devastations of World War II, and to promote peace for children worldwide, a project still pursued by the foundation that runs the two museums.

The museum was established in 1977 in the ward of Nerima to display her works, as well as to showcase the art of the picture book, which plays such an important role in the education of children. The general collection began with the acquisition of Eric Carle's 'Rooster' and includes over twenty-five thousand works by an international array of picture-book artists. The exhibitions I saw honoured Roger Mello (Brazil) and Shinto Cho (Japan) and – to commemorate seventy years of (relative) peace – Chihiro Iwasaki's 1973 book *Children in the Flames of War*. The museum itself harbours its own green secrets. Constructed in four spatially disjunct wings (two are two-story, two one-story) linked by walkways, it protects two gardens between the window-walled modules. So whether you are eating lunch in the café, opening books in the library upstairs, or noting the titles of books on the shelf next to Iwasaki's desk in her atelier, you are constantly tempted to look outside. (She was especially fond of the poet Kenji Miyazawa, the early-twentieth-century Buddhist poet who observed of Bashō's *Narrow Road to a Distant Province*, 'it was as if the very soul of Japan had written it'.) And there you will find 'Chihiro's garden' planted with the flowers she used to tend in her own garden, and which still bloom perennially in her illustrations, often with children looking out through dark eyes, all black iris and pupil, taking in the world.

Starting again from Shinjuku Station, you can go south past the vast expanse of Yoyogi Park and stop just north of the suppressed Shibuyagawa, at Harajuka Station, and walk over to the Meiji Jingu Shrine. Though I went there on the winter solstice it was a lovely warm sunny day, and the red-gold star-leaves of the maple trees gleamed through the dark green of the great forest planted after the war: 120,000 trees of 365 species (one for each day of the year!) donated from all over Japan. One walks to the shrine by passing under two of Japan's largest *torii*, enormous gates fashioned from seventeen-thousand-year-old cypresses. As you go under, you should pause and bow. The shrine itself, also built of cypress wood, is an example of highly refined Shinto architecture in the Nagare Zukuri style, with an asymmetrical gabled roof. It was constructed in 1920 to commemorate the Emperor Meiji (122nd Emperor of Japan) and his consort Empress Shōken, and was reconstructed after the war in 1958. The main shrine is flanked by the Inner Shrine, the Outer Shrine, the Treasure House, the Consecrated Kitchen (for the preparation of food offerings), and the Noritoden, where prayers are recited.

Emperor Meiji (1852–1912) was known for his efforts to reform and modernise Japan during what is known as the Meiji Restoration: he introduced the Meiji constitution, established parliamentary institutions, renewed diplomatic relations and trade with foreign countries, and encouraged education. (The preceding Edo Shogunate had closed Japan in on itself.) The Empress was known for promoting women's education and welfare, and for establishing the Japanese Red Cross. (Thus Tsuda College, the Bryn Mawr of Japan, was founded in 1900 by Umeko Tsuda, who in fact attended and was inspired by Bryn Mawr College.) They both wrote many poems in traditional Waka form, thirty of which are displayed at the shrine. On the way back to the train station I visited the Inner Garden, whose tea house looks down on the South Pond; I could only imagine the splendour of the iris garden, which blossoms in May, and I did not encounter any of the fairies of Shibuya, though I was serenaded by many of the denizens of the Bird Sanctuary just south of the pond.

Less than a half-hour train ride away from Tokyo lies the seaside town of Kamakura, arrayed along a winding road among hillsides stepping down to the sea. It is home to many Buddhist temples and Shinto shrines, as well as the Great Buddha (Daibutsu), which is a national treasure. I went first to Engaku-ji Temple, the main temple of the Engaku-ji sect, part of the Rinzai School of Buddhism. Tucked away between steep hillsides, it was founded in 1282 under the patronage of Hōjō Tokimune of the Kamakura Shogunate (who had just repelled the Mongolian invasion with the help of a typhoon), by a Zen priest newly arrived from China, Mugaku Sogen. Due to fire and earthquake, many of the structures have been rebuilt: the Main Gate was rebuilt in 1785, the thatch-roofed Mausoleum in 1811, and the Main Hall in 1968. There is also a Hermitage and a Zen Meditation Hall. Just down the winding main road is the Shokozan-Tokeiji Temple, founded in 1285 by a nun named Kakusan-ni, the widow of the regent of the Kamakura Shogunate. It was an (unprecedented) sanctuary for women seeking a divorce: a petitioner could obtain a divorce if she spent three years inside the temple. The temple fulfilled this purpose throughout the Edo Period, and then in 1873, women in Japan finally obtained the legal right to divorce.

Buddhism arrived in Japan, via China and Korea, in the sixth century. The Buddhist temples gleam inside the dales in shades of grey, brown, and pale green: wooden columns and walls, thatched roofs, copper plated roofs, stone walkways. But the Shinto shrines, like the Tsurugaoka Hachimangū that I visited next, are brilliantly painted, with dominant panels of deep orange and accents of yellow, blue, gold, red and green, which in early winter chime with the starry Japanese maples, the cloudy green camphor trees and the sky. The shrine was originally founded in 1063 but was moved to its present location by Minamoto Yoriyoshi in 1191; the next year, Yoriyoshi was appointed Shogun, establishing the Kamakura Shogunate, and precipitating a shift in the political centre of Japan from Kyoto to Kamakura. It was the first samurai (that is, non-aristocratic) regime in Japan, a supremacy that lasted 675 years, until 1867.

By the time I arrived at the Great Buddha it had begun to rain. I counted my blessings, because he is soon to be shrouded for half a year to undergo repairs. The construction of this forty-foot high, bronze Buddha began in 1252 and lasted a decade: the craftsman responsible for the casting was Hisatomo Tenji, but the name of the sculptor is lost. The halls which originally housed the Buddha were destroyed by wind or tsunamis successively in 1334, 1369 and 1498: since then, he sits under the dome of heaven, and his calm face expresses the Buddhist insight: the fact that we are living here, now, in the present, is the true meaning of existence; we are alive now. So I bowed as I left him, more or less in agreement, and went down to the seashore and gathered shells: rainbow nacre, purple and white, transparent and encrusted, spiral and oval. On another shore, Bashō wrote, 'Between wave and wave / Small shells mingle / With clover petals', among lines that evoke the book *Suma* in the *Tale of Genji*, and a poem by the twelfth-century Buddhist monk Saigyō.

Leaving Tokyo on the bullet train to Kyoto,

one may see Mount Fuji if weather permits, but it is never guaranteed. As my train pulled out of Shinagawa Station, I wondered whether my window seat was on the mountain side of the train. I was formulating my inquiry for the conductor ('Fuji? Fuji?') when suddenly, only about twenty minutes south of the city, as if I had called it up by naming it, the great volcanic cone, snow-capped and majestic, appeared on the horizon. I gasped so loudly that a couple of my fellow passengers turned, rather quizzically, to look at me; but it was as if I were seeing the Great Buddha again. Then it was obscured by hills and tunnels and gathering clouds, but just as the train passed by at the closest approach, the clouds parted and lay on the side of the mountain, harmonizing with the snow on its peak, shining darkly in the sunlight like bronze. And then it disappeared again behind the hills and tunnels; but I had seen it.

Japan is full of mountains, and even when you cross the southern plains there are mountains ringing the horizon. Just before arriving in Kyoto one passes by Bashō's Lake Biwa: biwa is a kind of fruit, a traditional Japanese guitar, and a lake: presumably they all share the same rounded contours. To the east of Kyoto's downtown, past the Kamogawa that along with its tributary the Takanogawa feeds a network of canals, lies the neighbourhood of Higashiyama under the kind green auspices of the hills that rise, steeply as always, on the edge of town. There my pilgrimage began with the Heian Jingu Shrine, another brilliantly painted Shinto shrine: orange is the colour that repels evil. Kyoto began its thousand-year career as the capital of Japan in 796, when Emperor Kanmu created it as the seat of government. He was the fiftieth emperor of Japan, and his reign lasted from 781 to 860: he improved the legal and educational systems, as well as domestic administration and foreign trade. The 121st emperor, Emperor Komei, was born in 1831; his reign was brief since he died at the age of thirty-six, but he laid the foundation for the Meiji Restoration. The Heian Jingu Shrine was erected to his spirit over a period of decades between 1895 and 1940.

If you leave the shrine and head past the Museum of Traditional Crafts and the Municipal Museum of Art (which I did not, alas, have time to visit) along the canal that flanks the Zoo – waving to the pink flamingos, giraffes and zebras – you come to the Nanzenji Temple, a Zen temple famous for its gardens. I stopped there for a cup of green tea, looking out through the open panels of the tea room at a mossy, ferny waterfall, and then continued to the Hojo Garden, where the sand is waved in river-like curves and a pine tree stands in one corner. The garden is dominated by a series of boulders whose conformation and arrangement give it the name Toranoko-watashi, 'Young Tigers Crossing the Water'. The interior panels of the adjacent building are decorated with beautiful scenes of birds and flowers, often against gilded backgrounds, but the most famous of these panels, by Tanyu Kano, depict 'Tigers Drinking Water'. There are in fact no tigers in Japan; Japanese tigers are conjured up by the arts of horticulture and painting.

To get from the Nanzenji Temple to the Ginkakuji (Silver Pavilion) Temple, one walks along the Philosopher's Path, which runs next to a canal and is decorated with abstract ideas, floating like the paper boats in Robert Louis Stevenson's *A Child's Garden of Verses* on the dark brown river with its golden sand, that flows along forever with trees on either hand. I felt right at home. It is named after a famous philosopher of the Kyoto School, Nishida Kitaro (1870–1945), who rejected the logic of Aristotle and Kant, and even the dialectic of Hegel. He proposed instead the affirmation of the absolutely contradictory nature of self-identity, life lived in an irresolvable tension between affirmation and negation, or opposed perspectives; he used to meditate as he walked along the canal. Where will all come home? The Silver Pavilion, halfway up another steep green hill, was established in 1482 by Ashikaga Yoshimasa, the eighth Muromachi Shogun. He owned the one-story Buddhist Hall, which is the oldest Shoin-style building in existence, its roof thatched with cypress. The adjacent building has two stories: the first floor is built in Japanese Shoin style, but the second floor is built, oddly, in Chinese temple style; a bronze phoenix on the roof, facing east, keeps watch below. There is also an observatory on the highest hill behind the temple, keeping watch as well, but upwards. At the end of my pilgrimage, I discovered that Kyoto is a good place to buy semi-antique kimonos and *obis* (sashes), quilted fish and dried flowers, and incense burners in the shape of boats and of tiny square ceramic Zen gardens, painted with one red maple leaf and striated like the sand-scapes raked into rivers.

The attentive reader will have noted an inconsistency in the histories recounted in Tokyo, Kamakura and Kyoto. Though the historians of the city prefer to fall silent on this point, Kyoto's domination of Japan was severely disrupted twice by the fierce warrior class that the aristocrats employed to stay in power. Between 1192 and 1333, two clans of Shoguns (the Minamoto and the Hojo) made Kamakura the military and political centre of Japan. A period of relative disorder followed, and then the Shogunate in Edo (Tokyo) assumed power, which persisted from 1603 to 1868. So the thousand years celebrated at the Heian Jingu Shrine were not unclouded; so too the history of Tokyo cannot really be understood without visits to Kamakura and Kyoto.

This inconsidency which was sorted out for me by a friend who lives in Komae City, where gleaming white high-rise apartment buildings loom over the floodplain of the Tamagawa, which only fifty years ago was embroidered with small rice fields. Here is the kanji for rice field, and so it appears on earth, in writing and in weaving.

I noted this pattern on a cloth another friend gave me as I was leaving Tokyo, I saw it from the sky as my airplane headed north, and I found it in a poem that Bashō wrote on April 20, 1689: 'A small field of rice / Just sowed; I left the shade / Of the willow.' The willow referred to a real tree by a 'pacing stream', which also flowed through a poem by Saigyō.

On my last day in Tokyo, I travelled by train and subway to the Roppongi Hills in the centre of the city, and flew up fifty-three stories by elevator to the top of the Mori Art Museum, capped by a sky-deck that offers a panorama of the city in every direction. The view of Tokyo Bay is especially wonderful. I watched a video that included views of Tokyo in ruins in 1945, and reflected that this city of thirty million people has recreated itself during the past seventy years, like the phoenix. I found a seat in the café next to a window overlooking the harbour, ordered a cup of coffee and a slice of peach pie and caramel ice cream, and finished writing my recollections of this busy city with its hidden moments of green, as the gingko tree above Bashō's vanished house dropped the last of its golden leaves. On August 11, 1689, towards the end of his *Narrow Road*, Bashō wrote, 'What was composed / On the fan is torn apart / And falls together.' I looked and looked for that tree in my neighbourhood near Bashō's house, but couldn't find it in the welter of streets and buildings from the long perspective of the sky-deck. Still, I knew it was there.

〜

My travels in and around Tokyo were made possible by the advice and company of many people. Many thanks to Professors Atsuko Hayakawa and Yoko Abe at Tsuda College, and their students Kei Yamada, Akiko Miyosi, and Saki Ogura; Professors Yoshio Yamasaki and Yasuhiro Oikawa and their students at Waseda University; Professors Masaki Harada, Takao Suzuki, and Fumihiko Takeda at Seisen University; at Kurumed Publishing and Café, publisher Tomoaski Kageyama, opera singer Erika Colon, film-maker Kazunori Kurimoto, musicians Kaori Muraji, Koko Tanikawa and Michiru Ohshima; at the Chihiro Art Museum, Secretary-General of the Chihiro Iwasaki Memorial Foundation Yuko Takesako, and Associates Yoko Nakahira and Yukiko Kubota; Yukiko Sazanami of the newspaper *Asahi Shimbun*; and friends and friends of friends, Tadatoshi Akiba (Former Mayor of Hiroshima), Yasuko Tsuka, Naoko Ogawa, Rieko Fukushima, Keiko Kondo, Kimiko Waku, Maki Ota, Kyoko Matsumura, Akiko Smits, Charlotte Eubanks, and Reiko Tachibana.

Four Poems

ROWLAND BAGNALL

Kopfkino

I felt lonely, like I'd missed the boat,
or I'd found the boat and it was deserted

Like the moment between knowing you might nearly jump
and actually nearly jumping, I considered half-undressing
an imagined Joan of Arc, approaching to the stake with unfaced
soldiers and a crowd of muted children like the children in the foreground
of a Lowry painting. The only thing she could get through to me was,
It's not that I'm afraid to die, I just don't want to be there when it happens,
which, given the circumstances, we all agreed was pretty funny.

It was one of those rare experiences where you move into rain that's already
falling somewhere else. In another place, but a place exactly the same
as this, I thought about the bit in *Fargo* (1996) where Steve Buscemi gets
stuffed into the wood-chipper until only his feet are left, imagining what that
must be like those first few seconds you're alive, and whether you'd bleed out
on the snow or just lose consciousness immediately, the way some people
suddenly lose consciousness when a roller-coaster hits a loop-the-loop.

Standing before Manet's *Execution of Maximillian* (c. 1867) in the National –
damaged into sections pieced together on a canvas in the 1990s –
I watched the shooting in full view, despite the missing fragments on the wall.
The Emperor clasped the hand of his companion as an officer, hardly visible,
signalled to the firing squad, vanishing behind a stage-effect of rifle smoke.
I decided that it was the best painting I had seen for a long time,
despite having seen it before somewhere, and missed it.

Someone laughed the kind of unexpected laughter that occurs
when you realise how ridiculous it is that you're disposing of a body
rolled inside a Turkish carpet, or hacked-to-bits and wrapped inside
a plastic bag to keep the blood from spoiling the upholstery in your car.
I could see a kayak heading for a hurricane, which was annoying
because I was in the kayak and I couldn't swim, or think of how
to get myself to shore. *Life is full of misery, loneliness, and suffering –*

and it's all over much too soon, I said aloud, which was annoying
because, given the circumstances, it would've been a lot funnier
if there'd been someone there to hear me say it. I could imagine
swirling around, not sure what it was that would actually kill me
but certain there'd be no way out of this one. As everything refocused,
like only realizing that someone has left a room when they re-enter it,
it was late afternoon and the sun was in my eyes so I hadn't seen anything.

Glider

for Peter Lanyon

Without knowing how, or why,
like trying to remember exactly where you were
exactly this time a year ago,
we allowed ourselves to be interrupted by
that interruption, as the launch cable detaches

from the substance of the ground below,
below the white and blue of the sea or sky,
a distanceless shape, opening and closing
with a kind of rushed completeness,
and if this was a kind of failure

what exactly did I mean by that? Like breathing
into a mouth which doesn't breathe back,
could you sense a delay between the two,
and how do you begin to distinguish that,
and even if you do, what do you get?

Making each time the same pattern
or the same pattern reversed,
everything was as we thought it would be,
except that nobody looked like they wanted
to be where they were, as if they'd simply

wandered into (or almost out of) the picture
by mistake, that line almost bending over

itself before it thins and rises up again
into a sword, if *sword*'s the word.
We stood there for ages,

watching it all accumulate, wondering
if there was a name for that which we'd forgotten,
without knowing how or why
the things we'd eventually agreed on
weren't exactly what either of us meant.

Sonnet

Eating at a restaurant where the food was all described as 'young' and 'tender',
you said that you had *absolutely nothing* to say, chewing chewing-gum.

Without looking at each other, I said, 'Did I ever tell you,' (knowing
I hadn't), and proceeded to tell the same old story, except that I couldn't remember

it properly, thinking for a second that it might have turned out differently,
which it didn't, which isn't to say I'd change a thing, trying to decide what colour

I'd call the ceiling if forced to call it a colour. On/After the day it happened,
something moved in the darkness and I stamped on it, all morning.

What would it feel like to undergo electrocution? What was/Was that
a hovercraft? Dissecting seafood, you explained how if you walk behind

someone on a deserted street you only have to quicken your step slightly
to instil fear in the person that you're following, or about the developing

technological capabilities of rendering the artificial 'real'. 'When you empty
water into a vessel and then shatter the vessel the water stays, just for a moment,

where it was, no longer slightly different from itself.' Was that blood
in the mayonnaise? I thought. Was that window blue on purpose?

Like a thought cut into speech, or black line next to nothing, everything echoes
and then the echoes meld, like unwittingly walking into a place you've just left

and not realizing it's the same place, or knowing why you've chosen to go in.
Can't you see a face? Can't you catch a brief glimpse from a passing train,

like the trains you can't see in a Hopper painting? On/Before the day it happened,
we watched that episode of *The Sopranos* (1999–2007) where Tony dreams

he's running from an angry mob and ends up riding on his horse inside the house
he used to live in with Carmela. You laughed the way you laugh when you're

not really paying attention, so I imagined you getting shot in an assassination
meant for someone else and went upstairs to hold on to the bathroom railings.

Without looking at each other, something moved in the darkness. Without saying
anything, I thought for a second that it could have turned out differently.

Drift

This happened to me and it didn't happen to me
or I spied it when I only heard it or found it

Put your fist through the exit wound,
if that's what you were doing. Sooner or later,
I removed the tablecloth without disturbing
the crockery, breathing through an apparatus
meant for keeping me alive. Was I Spartacus
as well? I thought, completely committed
to doing nothing except casually whispering
What year is this? to anyone who'd listen.

Going in at one end then out the same
way in with the momentary feeling that
something might be 'after us', it was difficult
to say precisely what was going on. A huge
second passed, unnoticed, if it even happened.
You said, 'The pattern of a thing precedes
the thing,' people moving off at incredible
distances in almost every direction.

Last Halloween, we saw two kids pretending
to be dead, a vampire and a vampire's brother,
(also dressed as a vampire), three separate
Spidermen and something like the alien from
Alien (1979) that was running up and down
the same street shouting something incoherent,
eventually instilling actual panic/fear into me,
the sallow ghost of Phillip Seymour Hoffman.

For instance: define 'hunger strikes', 'extra-
terrestrial', 'heart attack', 'gorilla masks'.
There was more we could've done, obviously,
wasn't there? 'It could be the worst thing
that's ever happened,' I heard someone
say, 'and if so, was it meant to be funny?'
trying to remember if *Blade Runner* (1982)
was set in Los Angeles or Tokyo, 2019.

Does that mean 'heart attack'? 'Sub-tropical'?
'Unremarkably'? Realizing simultaneously that
I was following footprints I'd already made,
I thought about a double-portrait that I'd seen,
completely forgetting, as it turns out, the names
of the people that it showed, imagining seeing
myself from all angles in a mirrored elevator,
unsure how many of the figures were still me.

Suddenly slightly out of focus but strangely
appropriate, like the soundtrack to a Quentin
Tarantino film, (e.g., when Mr Blonde dances
around to 'Stuck in the Middle with You'
as he's cutting off that policeman's ear in
Reservoir Dogs (1992)), everything was pressing
together and then skidding away hysterically,
seeking us out only to carry on ahead.

As though a change in the wind had enabled
us to hear a conversation that was taking
place some distance away but which no
longer seemed important, there you were
at the edge of the frame. *Did you catch that?*
Or that? Or did you just stop short in the middle
of a sentence and wander away, minding your own
business? And here: a hand grasping for air

from the window of a moving car. And here:
'a huge second passed, unnoticed,' the radio
cracking like a Frank O'Hara poem, (e.g.,
'Meditations in an Emergency'). It was difficult
to say precisely what was going on, completely
forgetting, as it turns out, if that's what you
were doing, so 'Put your fist through the exit
wound,' you said, from some distance away.

twenty love poems after Paul Verlaine

love version of

tonight I watched you sleep
naked on the futon
face down sweaty like a small child
and knew that everything else was bullshit

it's so hard to stay alive these days
or sane
so keep on snoring danny
while I guard you like a rottweiler

being in love with you is fucking awful
cause one day you'll stop breathing
in this grey light you already look dead

but then you smile thank fuck
what are you dreaming about baby wake up
tell me if the word soul still means anything

blue-screen

your grindr profile is an emoticon paradise
where camels and kittens go
dancing and flashing but I can tell they are :-(
beneath their primary colours

your preferences brag in arial bold
SINGLE / PASSIVE / NO STRINGS FUN
but they don't like themselves
so melt back into the blue-screen

into the silent blue-screen blank and sad
that makes the emoticons dream within their
programming and code run like teardrops
C C++ sob beneath your touch-screen

pastoral

above vauxhall the sky
is super blue
bus minutes click down
FIRE empties out

a fat pigeon burps
its coo of loneliness
shits
the sauna vents sigh

fuck me everything
seems so simple this early
the square mile soho boyfriends
asleep over the river

and you what have you done
standing there on a come down crying
tell me how many men
came inside you last night

other people's dreams are boring

I dreamt I was at chariots last night and
two lads
one blue-eyed one black
slipped out of the bleach-stinking steam

you should have seen their towels
damp with sweat hugging their smooth waists
smothering thighs flanks
cupping the dangerous meat between their hips

they pulled me into their labyrinth of clouds
terrycloth swaying like silk ball-gowns
on some ITV drama about adultery or longing

there in the wet room tiled like an abattoir
these boys opened their towels like the velvet
        curtains at an opera house
and I opened my mouth to sing

heath

the moon bleeds
light onto the black ash
every branch
in this dismal canopy
rasps indifference

like an ex-boyfriend

the salt marsh
is full of drowned things
the walnut trees
beckon like trade
the dark moves

no you are not dreaming

this desperate place
this scrub
cold
as dead starlight
violet

is your home now

like to go for long walks

I was always bimbling about KT3 SW20
looking down each suffocating avenue
for someone just like me

every driveway every park bench
every public lavatory
was an x might mark the spot

remember those pre-grindr days
when loneliness stung like a hunger
and you wanted to give yourself away like a milk tooth

homo do you still walk until your shins ache
up turnpikes across spaghetti junctions
through industrial estates along the towpath

your only treasure map
the salt-flesh wall in your stomach your semi

hackney central

what kind of slob leaves a used mattress
on the street tide-marked with
sweat piss blood and is that maybe cum
I swear you can see his outline in bodily-fluids

and he's not alone
four knees four palms four buttocks tattoo
the damp quilted magnolia cotton
they sure had a happy horny time of it

so what happened
did they move to hastings or get a swanky new one
the DFS memory foam 900

or did all that sex turn into regret
hell I know something about regret I've been
chucked away often covered in hickies sex-bruises

everyman

he's in the wank
bank this guy this hot
stranger who I've never seen
my shape-shifting cutie

I shut my eyes he wears the face he
knows I need yup he gets me
doesn't pity me like the others or sneer
just gets on with the job of kissing my

will he be blonde ginger
I can't say he chooses
his name is what was it his body is

built from grecian heroes
soldiers fishmongers pornstars slaves
yup he always gets me hard

stupid love

violin music
hurts my gut
like a punch

I'm always
thinking about
what happened

then crying
wish I could
leave you

blow off
like an old
carrier bag

:-(

your sleeping body grosses me out
puny submissive and bent
beaten by black dreams tattooed by crumpled linen
lucky I get turned on by weakness

sweating like you're running a fever
you shiver like a tot
your feet covered in gorgeous blisters
your neck bruised and slack

and your chest still bears my fist marks
and your mouth is an open wound
man you're a pathetic fuck

your brown eyes have shown me pain
then begged for more in silence I
wanted to know how much a man's body could take

scape

wimbledon's a sour & silly place
where I take my boyfriends to meet dad
fucking hate it when they say how pretty oh how quaint
the burnt yellow common the stagnant lake
the bone-white windmill that never turns
I clam up don't say this is where that group of lads
beat the shit out of me or this is where I lost it
to a bald guy without a condom or
this is where I used to wank sting my legs on nettles or
this is where my dad took me to say sodomy
ends in disaster

spleen

I never gave you roses
just black looks see

towards the end I was always on 50mg of something or other
blurred vision the shits

this fucking eerie sense of calm
the sky always through a lens of tears

without you I'm gonna stay indoors
foil over the panes become a shut-in a lifer

I've got plenty of pot-noodles
cup-a-soups chick-peas in my basement

been collecting batteries for currency
miss just one pill and I get crazy fearful

travelogue

the plain goes on
forever the snow
could be sand could
be moon-rock

the sky is beaten
copper the sun
lives and dies
each day like us

trees are moving
within the fog
something lives here
something survives

the sky is beaten
copper the sun
lives and dies
each day like us

and you my savage
starving shouting
into the north wind
how do you live here

the plain goes on
forever the snow
could be sand could
be moon-rock

autumn manifesto

the sun turns red and we're happy
blood everywhere the trees are roman candles
rivers silt up ponds soup
I get in line for my flu jab

it's our time of the year poets come
let's write our empty metaphors moan
about the rent crisis bovine
antibiotics in cheese syria

children and christians harp on about
spring the start of things they go a-picking
snowdrops and garlic yawn

but us poets we dig this red season
with its bonfire breath come let's put our scarves on
walk to the food bank

invertebrate

in the cave
where you fucked me
all these seashells look queer

this one's a bruise
with blood from your heart
your hard-on

this one's a salt-crystal
tears cum drying
on your cheek

this one's curly
like your ear this one's
peach-freckled like your neck

but this one is blade-sharp

vice

in advance of his trial for the attempted murder of Arthur Rimbaud, Paul Verlaine underwent a physical examination during which the prison doctors recorded finding 'traces of habits of pederasty'

sorbet-green smocks oxygen the sky through a hole and my legs are in the stirrups funny to have an audience yes funny for them to have clipboards pencils equipment this is the test you have asked for yes this is the test I have asked for you will feel pressure cold and I do and they scribble distended truncated and I wonder does the body bend or does the body break fuck I am chock full of the evidence of vice there is a gauge on my cock and a hand on my balls and I am a bull at market fraying towards its free extremity the crown stout nondescript go all the mouths and my heart beats like a lyre in my chest and I'm in the sky that is the colour of his irises only a lover should see you on all fours still I'm weighed judged like the organs of a cadaver surely flesh is just natural but the mouths go bears on his person traces of habits of pederasty active and passive oh how I remember both with glee and when I am sure they can't see me I beam like a boy into my hospital pillow

tindr

blonde or brown-haired I swipe the screen
blue eyes
or green I swipe again looking for another
with a poet's eyes but a short back and sides

soft belly hard abs lean I swipe the screen
heart
desperate or damaged who cares so I
swipe again there's far too many of us

man-slut or boyfriend material left right
yes no
does it matter there's always another
each fitter than the last each newer

green

here's a plastic basket of polyester tulips
plus a heart-shaped card that sings I LOVE YOU
don't recycle them please
be happy with my pound-store presents

I stink I'm pretty sweaty I've been walking
this whole damp night to get here
let me curl around your converse cat-like
and dream of our cherry days

maybe I could put my head still burning
from the memory of your hubba-bubba kisses
on your broad chest just till I feel a bit better
perhaps grab some shut-eye while you doze off

today

memories what the fuck do you want
making a fat pigeon beat the air again
the copper sun roll back years
the yellowed woods chatter with decay

we were alone together him and me
drunk sad our thoughts coming down
he turned his black-look my way said
is this happiness his voice metallic

his voice which had been so green
like my mouth my body
how I kissed his peachy neck and thighs

yeah the first years are so ripe
when open-mouthed kisses fill the silence
that today is long

the hole

hope what is it be honest with me
you think it's desire a want
a wasp fizzing
for the gap in the window

are you sleeping at all
wine helps whiskey too
I haven't gone to bed sober for eleven years
I don't know any lullabies

tell me to fuck off
if you want sympathy is so pat
you just want him back him

walking through your brain neck
still smelling of davidoff cool water
that wasp is always thinking of the rose outside

....

A NOTE ON THE POEMS

'There are no ghosts, no gods, nothing secretly lurking in the temple of the poem.'
– Don Paterson

Paul Verlaine was an extraordinary man – a hard-drinking and hard-loving bisexual poet who yoyo'd in and out of Catholicism, self-destructive behaviours and lustful revelry. Why, then, do so many English versions of Verlaine's poetry come across as tempered, quaint, lacking in the relevant energy?

For a decade I've been fascinated by Verlaine's poem 'Clair du Lune' with its moonlit, mysterious sadness. The majority of translations or versions of this poem describe, without irony, fountains, teardrops, the 'soul', attending to Verlaine's immense lyric genius but, I feel, overlooking the conflicted, oppressed, bawdy drunk behind them. Verlaine's character and sexuality is cast as his vice (a word prevalent in the critical literature) and the poems as his attempt at lyric redemption. In my poems I wanted to leave space for Verlaine, the dangerously progressive homosexual who eloped to London with Arthur Rimbaud, whom he loved so violently that he shot. 'Clair du Lune' became my 'blue-screen', and its 'soul' became a Grindr profile, a non-corporeal, secular and queer equivalent space of self-projection.

If 150 years of Verlaine scholarship, versioning and translation have sought to un-queer the verse, then I wanted to breathe queer life back into it. My obsession with Verlaine began as a desire to translate; I called on online dictionaries and Google translate as I went, I chose to dispense with meter, rhyme and punctuation, and to write in free verse; but I soon felt myself creeping into the poems. Verlaine's life became mine and mine his.

I don't wish to claim that sexuality is trans-historical or that the poetry is uncomplicatedly trans-personal, but what began as a wish to immerse myself in the poems of Paul Verlaine soon became a cycle of love poetry responding to his ideas, arguments, struggles and experiences. If 'blue-screen' began life as a hugely loose and queer translation of Clair Du Lune, then soon the other poems became homocentric shadows, or 'after-poems', responding to Verlaine's key ideas 150 years later. I don't claim these poems as my own but rather they are a one-sided duet with an anti-hero of mine, who I firmly believe would have enjoyed this new century of Grindr, Chariots, frank openness and looming equality.

– R. S.

'Only to the Dog'

Meeting Ezra Pound in the 1960s

MICHAEL ALEXANDER

I saw Ezra Pound several times in that decade: first in Rapallo in 1962; then after T.S. Eliot's memorial service, in London; then in the later 1960s, in Venice. I also visited Brunnenburg in 1964 and '65. I have reported one or two of Pound's remarks to me in what I have written about his work.[1] Yet a fuller account of what Pound said on these occasions may be worth making public. What follows is taken from diaries and notes made at the time. It adds detail to what is already known rather than altering the general picture, but some of these details may have their own interest.

The purpose of my first visit to Pound, in 1962, was to ask the translator of 'The Seafarer' if he would accept the dedication of a book I had begun, to be called *The Earliest English Poems*. This had been commissioned by an English teacher of mine, Peter Whigham, who had introduced me, among his other pupils at Worth Priory, a prep school in Sussex, to some of Pound's 'Epitaphs':

Fu I

Fu I loved the high cloud and the hill,
Alas, he died of alcohol.

Li Po

Li Po also died drunk.
He tried to embrace a moon
In the Yellow River.

Peter Whigham was the subject of a commemorative piece I contributed to *PNR* 106. I had met my prep-school teacher again after leaving secondary school. Knowing that I admired Pound's 'Seafarer', and seeing that I was to study Old English in my degree course at Oxford, he commissioned me to make verse translations of a selection of other short poems in Old English. The resultant volume, *The Earliest English Poems*, was accepted by Penguin Classics and was published in 1966.

I had written to Pound at Brunnenburg, the castle in the Italian Tyrol belonging to his daughter, Mary de Rachewiltz, where I believed that he was staying. The poet's wife, Dorothy Shakespear Pound, wrote back: 'I opened your letter to my husband and am forwarding it to him near Rapallo, where he is staying with a friend. [...] The address to find him is 131 Sant' Ambrogio, Rapallo, Liguria [...]. At the end of Aug: he will have to have a second operation.' Rapallo is the resort south of Genoa where the Pounds had lived before the war.

So my visit was arranged, but I learned that Pound was no longer staying with his daughter and his wife in the Tyrol but with 'a friend' above Rapallo.

It was on a morning of late summer that I began to climb up to Sant' Ambrogio, a coastal commune just south of Rapallo. The path rises steeply through terraces of olive trees. I soon overtook an older Italian woman carrying a bagful of shopping. Ten minutes later she overtook me; the day was pretty warm. I found 131 Sant' Ambrogio, a small white house to the right of the path, below the white church. In the US Detention Training Center outside Pisa in 1945, the American poet had recalled, among other memories of England before the Great War, calling on William Scawen Blunt: 'to have knocked / that a Blunt should open'. He took some pleasure in reflecting that he had not then been troubled by 'the diffidence that faltered'. I felt some diffidence as I knocked, but Pound did not open. The lady who did open the door seemed Italian and I assumed that the syllables she now uttered belonged to the Italian language: *Mi stair bee o woove*. The vowels were Italian, but it turned out that the speaker was American. She introduced herself as Olga Rudge. What she had said was 'Mister Beowulf', adding, 'I presume.' (I had then no wish to translate *Beowulf*, and was used to hearing its title pronounced *Bay-*, not *Bee*-owulf.)

Miss Rudge made me welcome but explained that Mr Pound was in bed. I had not thought about how serious Pound's illness might be and knew nothing about his recent operation. I was indeed expected and had come a long way, but it was kind of them to welcome me. Miss Rudge had said, by way of explanation before opening the door to the bedroom, that Pound suffered from 'pressure of thought'. 'He never did speak much,' she added, 'only to the dog.'

I was admitted to a small white room with a bed and a chair. Through the window I had a glimpse of the blue bay of Rapallo, far below. Pound, who was seventy-six, looked much older than he had in the last photograph of him I'd seen, which had been taken on his return to Italy in 1958, reproduced on the cover of G.S. Fraser's excellent little paperback *Ezra Pound*, published in 1960. This showed an active, energetic figure who proclaimed that the bughouse was the only safe place for a sane man in America. Now I was face to face with the maker of the translations and poems I had admired. The head lying back on the pillow was fine, the face much wrinkled, the eyes milky and remote. He was tired, even frail, and seemed more aged than anyone I had so far met face to face in my twenty-one years. That face was to be much photographed but I was perhaps the first English visitor to see this drastically revised Ezra Pound, a Pound who 'never did speak much'.

---

1 *The Poetic Achievement of Ezra Pound* (1979, 1998) and *Sons of Ezra: British Poets and Ezra Pound* (1995).

My notes made at the time begin 'A firm hand-shake', then,

MA: 'Are you on the mend?'

EP: 'Possibly. One can't tell'.

MA: 'I bring good wishes from Peter Whigham.' [Whigham, a poet and translator as well as a teacher, had himself visited Pound in St Elizabeths, the Washington mental hospital where Pound had been confined from 1945 to 1958. Whigham had transcribed for Pound some papers of Randolph of Roanoke; and had argued for the poet's release.]

To this delivered greeting Mr Pound made no response. He gazed out of the window. The silence lengthened. I ventured the observation that it was quiet and peaceful up there in the house.

EP: '*Quiet*... and *peace*' – longer pause – 'do not mean' – pause – 'the same *thing*.' This was uttered wearily in his distinctive cadence with its marked pauses and emphases. The voice had its own unique American timbre. Its unforget-table character – and the Aged Sage aphorisms it uttered – came back to me from the three television interviews at Brunnenburg that D. G. Bridson had made for the BBC two years earlier...

Recalling the purpose of my visit, I asked Pound if he would accept the dedication of *The Earliest English Poems*.

EP: 'If you think... it can be done... without EIR-RONEIGH.'

~

Aphorism was Pound's favoured style of utterance – when he uttered. He once defined poetry as 'gists and piths'. He praised writers who did not tell you things you did not want to know, and famously cut *The Waste Land* down to half its original length. So if Pound's recorded *obiter dicta* read as a series of separate verdicts, that does not misrepresent the way he spoke – fifty years ago. This disjunct quality was a consequence of his focusing on one thing at a time and a wish to say one thing at a time and as clearly as possible: to say it, then stop.

Not knowing how to reply to 'without irony', I asked, 'Do you write much?'

'Very little.'

Eyes on the window, stony. These exchanges – Pound did not always answer – did not take many minutes, though the time seemed long to me, and probably to him. Sometimes his lips formed into a soundless whistle. The young do not immediately realise the effects a surgical oper-ation can have on the old, and it was only later, and gradually, that I understood that Pound was profoundly depressed. It was by now late morning.

Olga Rudge kindly asked me back to supper in the evening of the following day. Before going to dine with them, I had taken their advice and walked a few miles round the crest of the hills above Rapallo. On arrival, I presented my hostess with a bottle of Asti Spumante. 'But this is wine for a cele-bration, *capito*?' So there was nothing to celebrate.

At dinner, however, Pound was more cheerful. He asked how Peter Russell was getting on with his bookshop, and spoke of Boris de Rachew-iltz's book on African Art; and of Frobenius.

When Olga Rudge was out of the room I asked him about further Cantos. 'I've a few fragments, but I can't make much sense of them, and nobody else can.' Then: 'She's kept me alive, and no-one will thank her for it.' All the self-confidence had gone.

I had sent him the first two of my translations from Anglo-Saxon, the poems called 'The Ruin' and 'The Wanderer'.

EP: 'There's a start. The coherence is there. Several unambiguous phrases. Something valid. Complete, perfect.... Your *Baath* poem is very fine' [that is, 'The Ruin']. Well, if 'The Seafarer 'was a start, you...'[2]

MA: 'Will there be another operation?'

EP: Shrug. 'She *makes* me read to her.'

EP [on discovering that I was a Catholic]: 'St Peters was built with taxes. The Church makes that distinction, between a loan which yields profit, and a loan which does not yield profit. That being so, why are all the churches in Canada mortgaged?' I had no answer to this question, nor to Pound's next one: 'Do they [the English] know that Dominican magazine?' (*Blackfriars*.)

I was then asked whether, as I was a Catholic, I knew Fr. Desmond Chute, a priest in Rapallo, who had recently died. Chute had been a close associate of Eric Gill in the Guild of St Dominic and St George at Ditchling. EP spoke much of Fr. Chute, and of his 'very fine' portraits of Yeats, of Hauptmann and of himself. 'Great loss. *Requies-cat in pace*.'

(I did not know Chute. Those who do not meet many Catholics can assume that Catholics will know one another. Randolph Churchill is said to have asked Pope Pius XII, 'Do you know my friend Evelyn Waugh? He's a Catholic too.')

Olga Rudge asked after Jean and Peter Whigham, and Peter Russell, and Denis Goacher, whom she knew and liked. It was a good evening, although Pound had no suggestions to offer towards a BBC radio programme I was to make with D. G. Bridson, called *Ezra Pound's Provence*. He had disliked the BBC's performance of his short opera, *Villon*. He said that Murray Shafer had been 'inaccurate' on his music. He, Pound, had not been to England since 1938.

I asked him if Ford Madox Ford was unhappy. 'No, not in his heart, though he had good reason to be.' Ford had come to Rapallo a few times. 'Who did his daughter marry?' I did not know.

Olga Rudge was learning to cook. Pound, always said to have been a good cook, has a line in the *Cantos*, 'Some cook, some do not cook, some things cannot be altered.'

OR: 'Am I improving?'

EP: 'You complicate things sometimes' (smile).

OR: 'All right Ezra, draught Ezra, coat Ezra,

2 I am grateful to David Moody, Pound's biographer, for tell-ing me that at about this time EP had written thus to a friend: 'Young Alexander has been irritated into doing better with anglo saxon....' In 1966 Pound wrote: 'Dear Alexander / thank you for excellent work & result in "Earliest English Poems" / I have just received the book and read the introduction. Yours cordially, Ezra Pound'. Olga Rudge wrote that he was 'Read-ing "The E.E.P" with great pleasure – Read poems out loud last night – nearly an hour ...'

woollen hat, Ezra, why won't you come out, Ezra, What shall I do, Ezra?' (All this called out from the kitchen).

EP: 'What do you think of Lowell? I read him more than I read some others. *Imitations.*' I said that I liked Lowell, but that he flexed his muscles too much. Grunt.

I found that EP did not know Ford's book *Provence*. I told him that I thought that his line, in the *Cantos*, that Ford's conversation consisted 'in *res* not in *verba*' did not strike me as obviously true. He fell back on *Se non è vero è ben trovato*.

I asked him whether he had visited Greece? He thought he would never get there. I suggested flying. EP (heavily): 'I have only *once* been... in an airplane.' [This was when he was flown back to face trial in Washington in 1945. He was to visit Greece in 1965.]

MA: 'Do you read Eliot's later work with as much pleasure as his earlier?'

EP: 'If you can take your pleasures *sadly* enough.... I don't think it amounts to very much.' (When Pound later told us all to 'READ HIM', he was probably thinking of the earlier work rather than of *Four Quartets.*)

On Eliot: 'If your grandfather has founded a university, the cultural level in the household is higher than if you come from nowhere.'

'I set out to be more cheerful' (than T. S. E.).

I defended Eliot, and confessed that William Carlos Williams wrote so much that I couldn't like it all – bad and good so mixed up. e e cummings also.

Did he read books about himself? EP: 'Kenner. *Gnomon* got it all.'

I defended Milton's prose. 'No.'

MA: 'You don't change your opinions'. EP: 'No, that's not true.'

He did not refer to the war, nor to Washington.

EP: 'Goodbye, sir.'

OR: 'Come and see us in the Spring.' She was glad to hear me talk, it reminded her of Adrian Stokes.

~

A second visit, in 1963, from Perugia where I was learning Italian, was also of a couple of days and also in the summer. This time I came to the little house above Rapallo with a friend, Martin Gray, riding pillion on the back of Martin's Lambretta, a two-day trip; I remember a very uncomfortable night on a park bench in Florence. There were several other visitors, friends of Olga's. EP's health was now better. Notes of my second visit show that he said 'I sleep like a hog' and that he felt better with every fortnight that passes: *ogni quindici giorni migliore.*

My impression was that he did not find the company interesting. A talkative musical friend of Olga's was visiting: Gloria Ramsey, from California. Olga, who had had a distinguished career as a violinist, was always trying to get people into the house in the (often vain) hope of stimulating EP. But Olga herself must have needed people to talk to.

MA: 'How are you keeping?'

EP: 'I get stupider and stupider.'

MA: 'Do you get enough time to yourself?'

EP: 'There's a fairly steady stream' [of visitors].

MA: 'Are there any more Cantos?'

EP: 'There are some fragments. I can't make sense of them and I doubt if anyone else will' [No change from 1962].

'I never studied anything seriously.'

'I know a little about the Malatesta.'

'When I got to the end of the 7th Canto I had no idea how to proceed.'

'I *loathe* fish.'

'There is no need for complete despair.'

'Of course, if you know nothing about books and you know nothing about life... if you're completely ignorant in both fields....'

'*Tempus loquendi, tempus tacendi.*' This, or rather the last two words of this, was now Pound's watchword, and often his response when asked for a public statement. It reverses a verse from the Vulgate version of Ecclesiastes, the third chapter, the one which begins: 'To every thing there is a season, and a time to every purpose under the heaven: a time to be born and a time to die.' Verse 7 ends 'a time to keep silence, and a time to speak'. Pound, the only child of a Bible Christian family, would certainly have known the next two verses: 'a time to love and a time to hate; a time of war, and a time of peace. What profit hath he that worketh in that wherein he laboureth?' That question is one that pressed on him: whether his life's work was all vanity.

These visits to the poet and translator whom I had much admired had turned out well enough in the end. Yet I resolved that I would not trouble Pound again; I had learned so much from his writings, and I might now learn from his silence. I could see that Pound (unlike Olga Rudge) did not want visitors. But there was much that I did not know.

~

BRUNNENBURG. In the summers of 1964 and 1965 I spent two holidays at the castle of Brunnenburg, staying with Peter and Jean Whigham and their young family. Whigham had moved the family there from Worth Priory. The Benedictines at Worth had decided to turn their preparatory school into a secondary school; at which, having no degree or teaching qualification, Whigham was not qualified to teach. What might be called his Fu I / Li Po tendency may also have played a part in his departure, I do not know. My former teacher was now nearing the end of his translation of Catullus, which was also to appear in Penguin Classics. The editors of the series had begun to admit the possibilities of a Poundian approach to translation. Whigham's stylish improvisations were very far from the 'readable modern English prose' which had been E. V. Rieu's policy for the Classics.

Peter and Jean Whigham and their family were staying in Pound's old flat at the castle, with furniture made by Pound, Gaudier-Brzeskas on the walls and the giant Gaudier head of Pound taking up a sizeable chunk of the castle's little triangular garden which looked down on Merano and the valley of the Adige. During these two holidays I met Mrs Pound – Dorothy – and Pound's daughter Mary, and her husband, Boris de Rachewiltz. Their castle, which has a fine position to the side of Tirolo di Merano, had been a very neglected building when they had bought it. The Whighams had no hot water in their flat. At Brunnenburg I met Noel Stock, the Australian disciple who was sorting out Pound's papers and would later write the first reasonably full life of Pound. Also resident was the amiable American philosopher Daniel Cory, who had been George Santayana's secretary, and others, including Peter Goullart, a Russian who had been a Buddhist monk in China. (Goullart, on being told by his London editor that the page-proofs of a book of his were too long by a few pages, and that they needed to be cut, cut out the requisite number of pages with a pair of scissors.) Much later I was to meet Dorothy's son, Omar Pound, and saw Dorothy herself in London, and met Agnes Bedford, Pound's old friend from Kensington days.

At our first meeting at Brunnenburg Dorothy Pound asked if I was reading Céline. I confessed that I was reading P. G. Wodehouse and had not heard of Céline. Dorothy, an English lady with a very straight back, discussed with me my translation of the Old English poem, 'The Wife's Complaint'. The wife, in that powerful monologue, lives in an underground cave, which must have recalled for Mrs Pound the unhappy days when she had lived in a basement in Washington D.C. to be near her husband in St Elizabeths. The wife in the poem is 'estranged, alienated – we lived each / alone, a long way apart.'

> Some lovers in this world
> live dear to each other, lie warm together
> at day's beginning. I go by myself
> about these earth-caves under the oak tree.

When I left Brunnenburg, Dorothy Pound gave me two of her watercolours.

Pound was not at Brunnenburg. I had read G. S. Fraser's little book and Hugh Kenner's first book on Pound, but only after I had read Stock's 1970 biography did I have a fuller picture of Pound's life and of the public record. The nature of his Rome Radio wartime broadcasts was becoming known in England. I was obliged to accept the evidence of what had previously been hearsay, that Pound had in these broadcasts been grossly anti-Semitic.

To read in cold print the selection of the broadcast texts, in the edition of Professor Leonard Doob, is a dismaying experience. Those on literary topics are characteristically – idiosyncratically – excellent. Others break down into incoherent abuse and manifest irrationality. These passages would certainly qualify as what is now called hate-speech.

~

WESTMINSTER ABBEY, 4 FEBRUARY 1965. I greeted Ezra Pound after Eliot's memorial service in Westminster Abbey, the first of three people to do so. After the service I saw Pound, standing in a long black coat, with a cane, outside the west doors, in a space apart from the many others there. Seeing that no-one approached him, I did so, gave my name, shook his hand and retired. He stood there on that cold day for several more minutes till two men approached him. The first said 'My name is Stephen Spender. I came to see you in St Elizabeth's. I don't know if you will remember me.' EP: 'No.'

The second man then identified himself as Cleanth Brooks, and as the cultural attaché at the US Embassy. I knew of Brooks as a scholarly literary critic of unusual quality. Brooks read out a public tribute to Ezra Pound's achievements, a tribute which he must have prepared in the knowledge that Pound was attending the service. It seemed to me an act of reparation on behalf of the American government, probably Brooks's own initiative. But few people will have heard it and Pound made no response.

Eventually a black car drew up, a car which Olga Rudge must have arranged, and Pound got in with her. As the car began to drive away a man started to bang on the car. I asked him what he thought he was doing. He said that he had handed Pound a card as Pound entered the Abbey, requesting an interview afterward. He was indignant. So was I: I thought it natural that, after attending a memorial service for one of his oldest and most loyal friends, and a lifelong supporter, Ezra Pound should have no wish to give an interview. The journalist could not see this. I argued with him for a few minutes. He had interviewed other poets in the *Sunday Telegraph*, and Pound was to be the third interview in a series. Pound had let him down, it would be bad for his career.

He thought of a remedy, however. A fictitious 'interview' duly appeared in the *Sunday Telegraph*, concocted out of what I had said to the man, padded out with remarks Pound was supposed to have uttered outside the Abbey, including such un-American vacuities as 'Eliot weather, this.' The wretched hack had made it all up. I telephoned the paper several times to protest, but to no avail. Eventually, however, after a letter from Stephen Spender, the paper had to print an apology. Many years later, in the late 1990s, I was seated opposite Mrs Eliot at a luncheon at which the T.S. Eliot Poetry Prize was awarded to the Australian poet Les Murray. I told Mrs Eliot about what I had seen outside Westminster Abbey, and she told me that when the date of her husband's memorial service was announced, Pound had written from Italy to ask 'whether if he came to London, he would be "*received*"'. This could, of course, be just a conventional way of asking if he might call on Mrs Eliot, but that is not how I take it.

After the service, Mrs Eliot had welcomed him to the flat and had tried to cheer him up. It is well known that Ezra Pound had apologised for 'that shit about the Jews'. It is well known too that in the remorse and depression of his last decade he very often expressed profound doubts as to whether his work had any value.

Pound is not the only writer to have doubted the value of his work, of course (see Ecclesiastes 3:8). But that he should hold himself so utterly disgraced that he had to write thus abjectly to the widow of his old friend I find very sad.

~

VENICE. A year or two later, on holiday in Venice, I was sitting on the Zattere, and looked up from my coffee to see Pound walking with Olga Rudge, between my café and the Giudecca canal. I again went up to present my respects, again intending to retire, as I had on the *parvis* of Westminster Abbey. But Olga Rudge took my arm and insisted that I come back with them to her little house nearby in San Gregorio, in the hope of amusing the old man (a hope not fulfilled). The three of us ate a couple of meals out at restaurants. Pound said very little, though he had not lost his wits. He was listening, but it was still *tempus tacendi*. At Olga's house I met Joan Fitzgerald, the American sculptor, a loyal friend and supporter of the frail poet and his strong companion. Joan, who had made a fine head of Pound, became a family friend, and we often met later.

Olga Rudge wanted to keep Ezra amused, anything to interest him or draw him out. He half resented it. She talked a good deal: I remember her saying that when they went to England to Eliot's memorial service, their bags must have been opened. Her remarks were usually followed by *capito?*, a rhetorical question expecting the answer Yes. She was always trying to get Pound to talk, or to eat, or to drink, efforts which met with much resistance. But the end of the Cantos records his profound gratitude to her.

~

In writing up these notes I have kept hindsight and comment at bay as far as I could. Thus I do not explain the identity of everyone whose name came up in these conversations. Readers of Pound will know of his relations with Carlos Williams, with Ford Madox Ford and with Eliot. Those who have not heard of, for example, Adrian Stokes, can easily find out more about him.

Pound came to regret his racial thinking, his political folly and much else. He suffered twelve years in a mental hospital, but his sins had been serious, and his reputation suffered also, very badly as the twentieth century went on. I doubt that younger readers of poetry read him much: a great pity. Also, an omission of Ezra makes the picture seriously incomplete, as Pound had a great effect upon the way poetry was written. Many writers and readers have gained greatly from his instigations, explorations and translations. Between 1911 and 1916 especially, Pound's ascendancy among younger poets, and with editors on both sides of the Atlantic, made him, as his obituary in *The Observer* put it, the 'most important literary influence since Wordsworth'. W. B. Yeats, aged fifty, asked Pound, aged thirty,

to help him make the diction of his poems less abstract. Pound got Joyce published. Pound 'discovered' Eliot, and it was his championship which made Eliot turn from philosophy to poetry. In the thirties, Pound (like many others) decided that Italian Fascism was better for Italy than Italian parliamentary democracy; and went on saying so after 1936. An anti-capitalist, he also began his public attacks on financiers, especially international Jewish financiers. He diagnosed the root fault of our commercial civilisation as Usury, falling back in his last years on Avarice. But to scapegoat 'the Jews' for the ills of our civilisation, as Pound did, put him, in the public mind, on the side of the sponsors of the Final Solution.

Someone whose ideas or conduct we find repugnant can, however, write good poems. Samuel Johnson condemned John Milton's regicide politics, his hatred for religious authority and his 'Turkish contempt for females'; yet Johnson's *Life of Milton* testifies handsomely to the scale of Milton's achievement. Johnson thought Thomas Gray shamefully idle, yet praised his *Elegy* to the skies. The younger Romantics disliked the way their elders had turned conservative, but respected their work. We read to inform ourselves, not to confirm what we already think.

Nearer to our own day, George Orwell praised the writing of Eliot and Waugh, whose politics he abhorred. In his poem 'In Memory of W. B. Yeats', W. H. Auden addresses the question whether a man with strange ideas can write good poetry. Auden says that Yeats, a master poet whose attitudes to the occult, for example, and to the aristocracy were poles apart from his own, would now be punished 'under a foreign code of conscience'. Auden differed even more widely from Ezra Pound in his attitudes to politics, to the role of the poet, and to poetic form. Yet Auden, a social democrat of leftish and liberal sympathies, made a BBC broadcast on Ezra Pound's seventieth birthday in 1955, appealing for Pound's release from the mental hospital. The world of poetry, now smaller and more marginal than it was in 1955, needs this ability to see beyond difference and beyond offence – even the most serious offence.

Three Poems

SINÉAD MORRISSEY

Meteor Shower, Coastguard's Tower, Ballycastle

The town has long since lost
its playground of sandy children
to baths and dragons,

Scotland has flounced in its hem
and shifted itself back
over the horizon,

Gamera's been at war
with Tokyo's would-be
monster destroyers

for hours and still your father
lets you stay – guest
among our lamps and books,

the blood of two ports
alive in our glasses –
and when it's finally

properly dark, as if
launching a bird from the bowl
of his hands or morphing

into a horse, he opens a door
to a crumbling staircase
and up we troop to the roof

together, illicit
threesome without your sister,
to watch for meteors.

At first the tilt
of the planet's axis
is answered inside us –

we angle ourselves
at a slant
(though the roof is level)

then slowly straighten.
What was here in the morning
has gone – Fair Head,

Rathlin. We've stepped out
on the deck of a ship:
the lights of the marina,

of the hill-backed streets
(glowing a decorous
orange beneath us)

the ship's own hopeless
circumference in the blacked-
out ravaging sea

of everything else. The sky's
all glower and show –
the biggest thing

in the universe
because it *is*
the universe – and so

we look up, at last.
You laugh. As though
getting flattened

by its mineral
anvil were grace,
we can't get enough

of the curtains of clouds,
closing, opening,
and the stars in behind

shining steady as lighthouses
and yes, not once but twice
– there and then there –

dust on fire at the edge
of Earth's flaying atmosphere
scoring its signature.

You whoop and run and lean
against both of us
and look up again.

We have set
our inadequate table
and sat down

in our whitest shirts
and the guest
has come.

Colour Photographs of Tsarist Russia

Because of so much colour – purples greens and blues, yellow, copper, reds –
where we least expect it, Prokúdin-Gorsky's outpost villagers seem more like us
dressed up than like themselves, posing in a past bequeathed to them in snatches
rather than interrupted from the task at hand. The girls look mismatched,
overfitted, stuffed into what was left after the travelling theatre's costume box
got ransacked. Old at seven, elbows out and serious as tax inspectors,
in layered skirts so beetroot they could have been soaked in soup,
these three proffer china plates of forest berries in variegated shades –
iris, magenta, plum – which ricochet in turn as a kind of rhyme
off floral handkerchiefs, pleated aprons, buttons, blouses, cuffs
dipped in dyes we haven't seen the like of. They can't be comfortable –
or are they merely wilful, staying put on the wrong side of the century,
refusing to wear trousers? The cerise shirt on the back of the man
in the open-shaft iron mine, resting on his shovel, the barge haulers,
woodcutters and troops of riverboatmen in vests the colour of duck eggs
turn 'Volga Work Parties 1905' into a room next door we might briefly visit
where nothing would surprise us. Want to see my boots? asks a foreman,
tipping up one foot at a cocky angle. The headscarf on his wife ignites a meadow.
And if, because they're richer, living in a town, or in thrall to Queen Victoria
and her calamitous black, some people have fought back their spectral natures,
choosing instead to appear to us both looped-at-the-waist and dark, the buildings
behind them haven't: whole streets rise seashell-pink or powder-blue
out of the middle picture, ringing the radical bells of themselves for miles around.
Over *Golódnaya Stiep,* or Starving Steppe, the weather cooperates also:
this sky exactly half of what's been taken two shades brighter than lazuli
with no rain cloud in sight is as good as God's promise to Ishmael
for the women scything a hayfield underneath it. Tashkent, Archangel, Samarkand.
And he's stopped for moment *en route* – these days his perpetual state –
for a rare self-portrait: hatted, moustachioed, bespectacled, thin,
Chief Photographer to the Tsar. You can tell he's already distracted
by the thought of his railway-car darkroom (a gift from Nicholas himself)
where the three magic filters for his new magic lantern will approximate what was there.
This particular babushka on this particular veranda on this particular evening
in this particular summer is spinning a skein of wool. Tomorrow night is bath night.
In the morning, she'll step out of the clothes she owns including her footcloths
and into her second shift, boil a copper of water, slosh and sluice them clean
with a stick of birch then hang them out to dry all day, like the flags
of a continent's countries strung across her garden, so that afterwards,
her hair de-gritted and every pore alive, not a single unwashed item touches her skin.

Collier

1.

Though he never once placed a bet, my grandfather
sat in his chair every day and picked out winners:
Larkspur, League of Nations, Isinglass, Never Say Die

in the 2:30 at Epsom or Newmarket.
He'd follow their dips and peaks, ingesting the painfully
difficult newsprint on off-work afternoons,

or he'd rely on the tug-at-his-sleeve of instinct:
his grandmother's Romani nous with horses, his blacksmith-
father's apprising sense bred into his muscles and veins...

And so his damaged house filled up with winnings:
tickets to a race, pairs of boots to choose from,
a tea cosy from a shop, a pigeon cote out the back,

and after each spectacular nose-across-the-finish-line
outsider made him rich (which happened twice)
he'd sit and eat his wedding supper over again in his imagined

life: ham on the bone; salmon, roast beef, egg-and-cress; a cake.

2.

No matter the shift, the only food he'd take with him
down the pit was bread and jam, two slices wrapped up
in grease-proof paper, and a bottle of gone-cold tea.

He'd perch in a cranny to eat it half-way through
his eight-hour stint at the coal face, black as a bat
bar the whites and reds of his eyes and his teeth's gapped ivory.

Each mine an auditorium. Under the fallen sun
of his headlamp, like the ghost of the boy-he-was
at the sorting station sorting out nuts from brights,

he'd array the sounds the tunnels carried
– the squeal of the wheel, an invisible neighbour's cough –
discarding each in turn until, in his blue-scarred palm,

he held up gold: miners' saviours in cages singing their lack
half a mile off, back by the fluted shaft, singing
no black damp, no gas, until he'd sing himself.

He knew eight-and-twenty ways to raise the roof, some safe, most not.

3.

What possessed my granny, slim, smart, solvent, raising the roof
every Friday night after work at the Palais de Danse
in Nottingham, showing the band what-for with spies and soldiers,

to marry him? Some runaway freight car undid her, shunting her north.
Already his breath was a wounded animal pacing its ever-decreasing
circle underneath his rib cage. He couldn't afford linoleum.

The village had five shops. He was born in the reign of Victoria;
they'd finally buried the dead of Ypres before my granny
came caterwauling in. Once, as a child,

visiting her spinster-aunt's friend in the countryside
who kept house for her younger brother, she was privy to this:
a walking shadow, the size and shape of a man,

stole across the room towards the kitchen, not touching anything.
The kettle's whistle. Splashing. Singing. Then the shut door
opened abruptly and out stepped a white vest and a clean face

and the moon's penumbra vanished into brightness.

4.

Bright as a whitebell in Handley Wood, bright as the heads
of poor man's pepper shaking their throwaway lace
all over the lanes between New Whit and Eckington

was the evening he proposed (and the proud hart fleet
upon the enclosing hills and the honeycomb oozing honey).
And late the next day he stepped into a cage

and fell the length of a tarpitch mile, not looking, *yes,*
to where pit ponies stamped in their stalls, not listening, *yes,*
and was out along a by-line

dreaming his Skegness honeymoon into place
when a heaped tub of altogether coal, *yes you Tom Goodwin,*
yes, began snarling his name.

You might measure the force of its freak uncoupling
by what was crushed: it took an hour to manage the mess
of lungs and bones and blood to the surface.

He sat out in blankets and looked at the sea for his month at the Miners' Rest.

5.

A month at a Miners' Rest, alright, but no compensation –
every time she paid a coal bill, or dressed my mother
in a cousin's pinafore, my granny would preen and peck

at the elderly man grown elderly early
hunched across from her in his armchair.
He'd turn himself into a tree and wouldn't answer.

And the silence of Glasshouse Lane burred with thistledown
like a blanket sewn by swallows just for them
would settle over the room

and he'd light up a woodbine and smile until she smiled too
and then the damp-blotched ceiling would open
and in their last companionable hours together

they'd play host to strange familiar visitors
soft-landing expertly in amongst the furniture:
Eric Coates *Calling All Workers;* Ralph Elman and his Bohemian Players;

Ron and Ethel taking forever to get nowhere in *Take It from Here.*

6.

Because the distances you travel are unimaginable
to the man who flicks open each wing in a fan-card flourish
checking for balance and corkiness

before shunting you onto the train for your journey south
and over the freezing sea
towards liberation at Rheims or Poitiers

and because your tiny friable arrangement of magnets and air pockets
through which the planet articulates its cleverness
might be crushed by a falcon in an instant, but isn't,

and because your most exhilarating trajectory
is not just from darkness to light, as his is,
but from darkness to the upper storeys of the air itself –

coaxing you down off the toss from Bordeaux or Nantes
to the landing board, getting your leg ring clocked,
is to stand with a capful of coins in the Miners' Arms, a balloon adventurer,

or like a man who has tasted the rind of the moon, without ever leaving home.

In, Among, With and From
In Conversation with Thomas A Clark
ALICE TARBUCK

Thomas A Clark, *Hölderlin's Shopping Bag* (2014)

ALICE TARBUCK

You have described your work as being engaged with 'fields of enquiry'. These fields, to my eye, are usually formal, rather than thematic. What are your current 'fields of enquiry'?

THOMAS A CLARK

Well, I hope that they are both, since a poem is a braid of form and content. I suppose that I tend to think of the poem as an heuristic device, a question you can ask of the world, or a patch pegged out for closer examination.

We are all familiar with the experience of going for a walk but carrying all the usual baggage along with us. The poem can be one means of assuming responsibility, a commitment that you will stay alert to what is going on, outside and inside the poem.

I don't know that my 'field of enquiry' has changed so much, but 'enquiry' may be too solemn. 'Curiosity' may be a lighter way to think of it. For me, curiosity is inseparable from the impulse to make.

In a 1983 work, Three Triolets, *you visually delineate the structure of a triolet using coloured lines instead of words. The relationship between visuality and poetic form is central to your work – how would you describe that relationship and its evolution?*

The first Moschatel publications were printed letter-press and for years we worked with just two typefaces, Bembo and Gill Sans. It is not that these were two modes, exactly, but some things would look good in one and some in another, although it would be difficult to say why, a question of feeling rather than decision.

This did teach me that presentation might be an aspect of form. When it looked right, it felt right. If everything stretches out from the left margin and depends from the top margin, any departure from that is meaningful. When a few words are isolated on a page, you must read the space as well as the words.

Poetry is an art of movement and sound and I often want to work against the grain. Also, stillness and quiet offer a small counterweight to rush and noise, to a deliberately induced bewilderment.

Sometimes you make works that can be easily incorporated into domestic environments, for example Cumulus, *a one-word poem on a pillowcase (Moschatel Press, 2015). These works subtly alter the contexts into which they are placed. What is the relationship between text and object in these works?*

I notice that your question substitutes the word 'works' for 'poems'. It is understandable, but for me such works are all extensions of some formal possibilities of poetry. I think of them as poems, although the phrase 'poem object' might be an alternative.

In traditional poetry, no word is ever on its own. It always arrives within the context of other words and phrases, in the line or in a stanza. In poems that are off the page, a phrase or a single word may be placed within a non-linguistic context, a wall, a room, a wood, or embroidered on a pillowcase. The poem is not the word or phrase but the whole situation including the word or phrase. People who find that this does not have the richness of poetry on the page simply don't know how to read the context.

Peter Riley has described your poetry as 'grasping the fusion of image and abstract in real experience'. Does it ring true, that the fusion of concrete image and abstract thought is central to your work?

Mallarmé told Degas that poems are made with words and not ideas but I only partially agree. That the dawn wears a russet mantle or that so much depends upon a red wheelbarrow are images or concepts; there is no great verbal felicity to them. These examples also show that thought is not necessarily linear or sequential. It may be a kind of grasp, as Peter says. Or a lingering, like light on a stone.

How does using a variety of media affect the 'fusion of image and abstraction' – do they relate differently in Moschatel Press's printed work versus poem-objects such as Cumulus *or* intelligence *(2015)?*

Most reading still takes place in private, in imaginative rather than literal space. With the many cards we've published from Moschatel, the words and image are printed on front of the card, so the poem moves out of the book, out of literary into everyday space.

This is the beginning of the poem object, but I must emphasise that this is not a matter of simply printing poems onto objects but an attempt to rethink the whole relation of words to their context. It takes the old Williams notion of 'no ideas but in things' quite literally, but occupying all the prepositions; no ideas but in, among, with and from things.

Your series of plaques (e.g. quiet, *2015), are another form of small-scale installation art. Plaques are usually designed to draw attention to a particular spot: your plaques are paradoxical because their final location is outwith your control. What, for you, are the formal and artistic pleasures of poem-objects that sit at the border of print/sculpture/ poem?*

Sometimes I am commissioned to make something in a particular place or situation and then it is a question of what I might contribute that will seem appropriate and worthwhile. In a way it is no different from working in a line or a stanza; as the context develops, you try to find words that will fit into, or emerge out of, that development. The only difference is that here the context is supplied.

With the plaques, the situation is reversed; people have a set of words, a sentence or a phrase, for which they have to find a place. It is another form of reader participation. They are invited to practice an ethics of installation; if you place something in an environment or a culture, a poem or a melody or a building, what is its contribution, will it be helpful or disruptive, civilised or barbaric?

In a review of Ian Hamilton Finlay's work for PN Review *you say that the various media in which Finlay worked 'all have their sense of what is fitting'. Your work, too, seeks to create harmony between form and content. How do you understand 'what is fitting' in terms of the aesthetics of your work?*

On the whole, I don't place words in the landscape. Gardens are another matter. I am perplexed by much public sculpture, which demands that people turn away from the landscape in order to admire the art. When it comes to art in the landscape, the ethic of minimal intervention is surely appropriate.

It is no different within the line. I am usually concerned to assist the flow, or shift it or slant it, rather than to interrupt it. It is a matter of decency or comportment. Although I can think of some situations one might want to disrupt or undermine, the reading process is not one of them.

Your poetry explores the idea of paying close attention to the world. Do you think certain forms can help us attend to the world?

It used to be said of 'free' verse that it was just chopped-up prose, and indeed it is too often arbitrary and lazy. But the criticism can be turned around; if you write anything in continuous prose, in joined-up writing as it were, it can very quickly go flat; you begin to see how lineation can work against looseness, in its proper function of measure.

Indeed, your use of repetition and variation in particular is reminiscent of traditional Celtic poetry and song – one thinks of A Celtic Miscellany, *for example. How do traditional songs and poems influence you?*

In folk music and folk poetry, the element of play is often to the fore, together with an undiluted desire or retained wonder. That the line of a tune is its own fulfilment seems to me exemplary, an exercise of the breath or of the fingers or the arm.

It is not correct to think of this as naïve art, since the musicians and bards are fully aware of their place in a tradition. It does offer one alternative, quite outside the Western canon, to a literary modernism (modernism in the visual arts is different) that insists on difficulty and hermeticism, and is essentially critical rather than celebratory. In a collection like the *Carmina gadelica* there is so much affection for the natural world, a commodity in short supply in contemporary poetry.

Repetition is a coming home to the same, as old jazz bands used to say 'one more time', just for the hell of it, to hear the story or the tune again. Yet the same is never quite the same, since it retains a memory of the first time and hears or sees in that light.

Moments of pause are of central importance to your work: quiet- ness within your poetry, but also the pauses on the page, created through your use of blank space. What role does space and silence play in your work?

You already have it when you say, space or silence or quiet. In conven- tional lineation, the eye is pulled down the page. There is a certain compulsion about it, which I resist. If the poem is long enough it runs over onto another page; in other words, the page is there merely as a support for the words and makes no positive contribution.

With Mallarmé, the page begins to register. For him, the space of the page is white; it is a symbolist space, translating as snow, or a swan, or purity. For the concrete poets, space is structural, akin to the intervals or spacings in Derrida, which hold language or allow it to breathe, or differentiate, or build.

I do think that the vertical pull of lineation, together with a certain avant-garde practice of parataxis, whatever its intention, is too much in collusion with consumerism, with the continual inducement to move on. If something is worthy of mention at all, give it some space and time, stay with it, before moving on to the next thing.

In a book such as *yellow & blue* (Carcanet, 2014) the space between sections is longer than the stanza break. It is a break in discourse, potentially as long as the preceding poem, but it remains undecided whether these are separate poems or parts of a larger work. Their ability to stand alone and to link up raises a question, while it puts a brake on the forward impetus of narrative.

Thomas A Clark
quiet (2015)

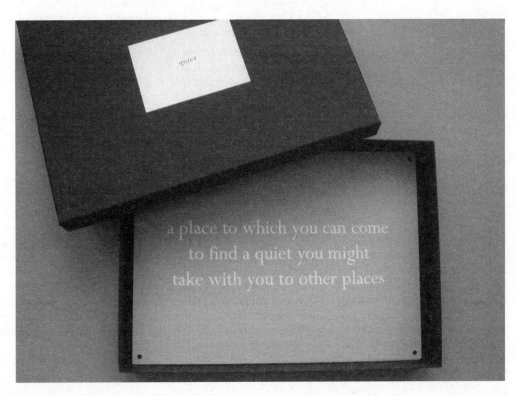

The 'I' appears only reluctantly in your work – usually the poems address the reader using 'you', if at all. Where 'I' does occur it is impersonal. Do you feel that your work supposes – or hopes for – a commonality of experience between implied speaker and existent reader?

The second-person pronoun is a 'shifter', less easily identified and pinned down than the first-person. It may be singular or plural, addressed to a companion, the reader, or the speaker in reflective mode. These are undecided at any moment and therefore allow space for the reader to be inscribed in the writing.

Actually, most of the content is personal, in that it begins from something in my own experience. But I don't want the reader to continually refer back to me. It should be the reader who walks in the hills, or follows a trace, or comes to a river. To read is to try on a series of imaginative variations that loosen and expand the range of sympathies. An opportunity is lost if it remains my experience rather than yours.

For this reason, so long after the 'death of the author', I'm puzzled by all those post-modernist poets who want to jump up in readings to be identified as the owner of their words.

Your work often uses techniques of emergence and immediacy, presenting the reader with an image rather than 'leading them in'. In your longer collections this creates coherence, within which each poem remains fragmentary. Could you speak about the tension between coherence and fragment in your work?

With the best will one can summon, attention is intermittent. The 'fragments' (or poems) are moments of attention, or of vivid appearance, while coherence is a thread through the fragments, or a sense of a journey, or the continuity of a terrain. You come to one thing and then another, on a walk or in a book. For the Romantics and the Modernists, the fragment was a site of nostalgia and decline, while for me it is a chance to wake up!

The idea of 'givenness' in the Husserlian sense can be applied to your work, I think, particularly works that detail images of the natural world stripped of their identifying particulars. What is the relationship of that 'givenness' to your poetry?

Everything is given to consciousness, which is itself given. The world is given, perceptions are given, and so too is language. These are evidence of an absolute expenditure, apparently without provenance. I don't share the cynicism, originating from Mauss, that giving is inevitably self-interested. We all have experience that giving may be as selfless as the gift of the world is authorless. The fact that poetry is without value, but is often received and valued, may be a satisfying approximation.

In English, we can play on the word 'present', as gift and immediacy. This has implications for making; if you want to make a present, you want it to be something good, the best you can manage, something the recipient might use or enjoy. You can keep the recipient in mind during the making. This is a different attitude from the one that sees the reader as someone who needs to be challenged, to be coerced or shocked into attention.

Much of my work attempts to be present in the second sense, of being immediate or there all at once. This is one reason for its often extreme minimalism, its reduction of moving parts.

I'm interested in the interplay between philosophy and humour in particular strands of your work. These works feel like a loose series on the phenomenology of reading. Would that be a fair observation?

One might say that poetry is itself 'a phenomenology of reading' in that it is always to some extent self-referential. Poetry is the art that draws attention to the material presence of language. If prose is a window on the world, poetry clouds the glass, as it were. Rhyme, metre, lineation, all draw attention to themselves, to function as a delay in the appropriation of a detachable sense. It can be done lightly, in a self-referential turn, or in a little dance or tune in the line.

In a recent interview with Luke Allan for PN Review, *Richard Skelton (Corbel Stone Press) mentioned that you advised him to 'live a creative life'. Your gallery, Cairn Gallery is at your home. How has this on-going relationship with, and space for, diverse artists influenced your work?*

One thing I've always liked about artists is their relaxed way with the working situation. It is no big deal. If that were carried over into poetry it might be less of a high artefact, an aspiration to 'literature', than just something made. Both the concrete poets and the Objectivists saw the poem as an object rather than a song, something quite separate from the lyrical self, put together with words. I go halfway towards them in that I like the finished, shaped object but I also like a tune, a slow air.

But what I particularly learned from artists of my own generation was to limit the field of enquiry, that there may be a consistency to making and thought, that you don't need to jump from one thing to another. This gives the possibility that a whole life's work can be one thing, the separate poems part of a corpus. By chance, I started working with artists about the same time that I came across Husserl and his idea of the phenomenological reduction seemed another way of focusing on a set of concerns, keeping everything else outside the brackets.

François Zourabichvili frames the relationship between self and landscape, saying: 'To live a landscape one is no longer in front of it, but instead, one passes into the landscape.' Your work often invites the reader to enter into the poem, into the imaginative space provided by the poem. What do you think the importance of these spaces is?

The book is a place apart, a complex, multi-layered space to move about in and explore. It can be a wee holiday. My work has been called escapist but the charge is itself complacent, failing to acknowledge that many people live or work in situations from which they would be glad to escape, if only for the length of a poem.

The typical reading circumstance is still one where you sit in your favourite armchair, open a book and go elsewhere, to climb a hill, pick blaeberries, stand in the rain or sit by a burn, then you close the book and are back in your chair again. This going and coming, embodied and disembodied, weighted and light, is refreshing. The hope is that, by means of this little detour or imaginative variation, you can come back to everyday circumstance more alert and resourceful.

Thomas A Clark, *Longing* (2000)

Sleeping with Gozzano

PATRICK WORSNIP

Agliè, Italy – Did Guido Gozzano die a gay atheist? For conservative Roman Catholics in Italy, that would be pretty bad – about as bad as you could get. Dante would be hard pressed to know which circle of Hell to put you in. The short answer, on both counts, is that we are never likely to know for certain. But first – who was Guido Gozzano?

It's a fair question. Outside of Italy, he is little known. Even within Italy he's hardly a household name. He is, says my Umbrian neighbour Piero, a retired diplomat, 'practically forgotten'. And yet Gozzano occupies a pivotal position in pre-First-World-War Italian poetry as the most accomplished of the so-called Crepuscular, or Twilight, group. He stands between the classicising greats of the nineteenth century such as Giosuè Carducci, Giovanni Pascoli and Gabriele D'Annunzio (though D'Annunzio survived well into the twentieth century, over twenty years longer than the short-lived Gozzano) and the moderns Giuseppe Ungaretti, Eugenio Montale and Salvatore Quasimodo.

My quest for Gozzano, as his *aficionados* prepare for this year's centenary of his death, takes me to Turin, capital of the northwestern region of Piedmont. He had an ambivalent relationship with the place where he was born, died, and spent much of his life, and yet it's difficult to imagine him anywhere in Italy other than here. Not the Turin of Fiat, Nutella and Juventus Football Club, not even the birthplace of Italian unification in 1861, but the city of casual elegance, with its arcades, tree-lined boulevards, ornate coffee houses and patina of French culture.

Just off the fine Piazza Solferino is the imposing building where Guido was born on 19 December 1883, a fact recorded by a plaque on the outside wall, which also says that, at his death, he 'reached God'. The Italian verb in the inscription, the work of his friend and fellow writer Carlo Calcaterra, is '*approdare*', literally meaning to make landfall. A mile or two away, in a less grand house in a less fashionable part of town (the family's finances had suffered after the death of Guido's father, a successful railway engineer, in 1900) is the apartment where he died on 9 August, 1916, of tuberculosis, aged just thirty-two. A tobacconist's on the ground floor faces onto the street. There's a plaque here too, which says the poet passed away 'with his mind turned to God'. You might get the impression from these two inscriptions that Gozzano was a deeply religious man. And yet at one time he had called himself an atheist. 'As you know,' he wrote in 1903 to a friend about to be ordained as a priest, 'I do not believe.' Which may be the unwritten subtext to the message the plaque-writers are trying to convey.

I have made contact with the Friends of Guido Gozzano, a Turin-based group whose vice president, Lilita Conrieri, has invited me to meet her at her flat not far from the city centre. It's a vast, old-fashioned apartment where, even if you stood on someone's shoulders in the living room, you still wouldn't reach the ceiling. Also there to greet me are her mother (who bustles about fixing drinks) and two friends and fellow Gozzano buffs. In her day job, Lilita is a paediatrician at a children's hospital in Turin. As I talk to her, I can't help noticing behind her the largest birdcage I have ever seen in a private residence, made of wood painted pale green and decorated with the emblem of Savoy, a territory which once covered parts of France, Switzerland and Italy. Lilita says it's nineteenth-century. I observe that there are no birds in it. 'There used to be some,' she says. 'But they went mad and killed each other. Maybe it was too dark for them.'

I am keen to know whether there are surviving members of the Gozzano family in the area, but Lilita says not. Guido had no children and the only one of his siblings who did was his elder sister Erina, but they emigrated, possibly to America, she says. The talk turns to the true centre of the Gozzano heritage, a villa named Il Meleto (The Apple Grove) once owned by his family just outside the small town of Agliè, about twenty miles north of Turin. Guido loved it and did much of his writing there. Built as a summer residence in the mid-nineteenth century by his maternal grandfather, it's now a museum dedicated to the poet and it's there that annual Gozzano literary awards, conferences and other events take place. As we talk, I suddenly grasp that the villa now belongs to Lilita's family. It was sold off with its land in 1912 with the proviso that the Gozzanos could have lifetime use of the house. But after they died out it gradually fell into disrepair, until Lilita's father bought it in 1972 and slowly restored it. It occurs to me that if there are any 'descendants' of Guido, they are in a sense Lilita and her eighty-eight-year-old mother (her father is deceased).

Lilita says Gozzano is known in Italy, 'but in a superficial way'. After performing poorly at school, he started legal studies at Turin University but preferred the literature lectures of poet Arturo Graf, who encouraged him to break away from D'Annunzio, an influence on his early work. His principal verse collections were *The Way of Refuge* (1907) and *The Colloquies* (1911, translated for Fyfield Books, along with selected letters, by J. G. Nichols, 1987), which contains his best known poems. The Crepusculars did not give themselves that name, it was coined by the critic Giuseppe Antonio Borgese in a 1910 newspaper review of three different poets, to whom Gozzano, Umberto Saba (not now considered a Crepuscular) and several more were later added by others. Borgese wrote that, for public opinion, after the great works of the past, the sun had gone down on Italian poetry. 'It is setting, in fact, but in a gentle and very long twilight [*crepus-colo*], which will perhaps not be followed by night,' he added. The Crepusculars, the Italian scholar Giuseppe Gazzola says, 'refused to play the role of laureate poets, to celebrate bourgeois pomp and convention, as Giosuè Carducci had done'. And for the American poet and academic John Frederick Nims: 'In reaction against the flushed heroics, sexual hysteria, and gaudy optimism of D'Annunzio, they deliberately swung to the other extreme: began to look at life wanly (but with irony) from garret windows, began to loll and droop in withered gardens, to dwell on sickness, and to yearn dolefully for *La belle dame sans merci*.'

Gozzano, Montale later wrote, sauntered into public prominence 'with his hands in his pockets'. He wrote of provincial life, his own uneasy place in it, and the frustrations and misunderstandings of relationships never destined to reach fulfil-ment. Gozzano's poetry, even in short pieces, 'is all narrative', said the poet and film director Pier Paolo Pasolini. 'If it's not a real story he's telling, it's still a 'scene' from real life.' In his irony, he has been compared to the French poet Jules Laforgue, and through him to T. S. Eliot. To me he has more than a hint of Philip Larkin and other poets of the Movement. When one of those, Kingsley Amis, wrote (in 1955) that 'nobody wants any more poems on the grander themes for a few years [...] At least I hope nobody wants them,' one can almost imagine Gozzano nodding in agreement. On the more positive side, Gozzano and his fellow Crepusculars set about bridging the gulf that had long existed between the language of Italian poetry and the language spoken on the street (I might make an exception here for Giuseppe Gioacchino Belli (1791–1863), whose poems, some of them very rude, were written in Roman dialect). Gozzano combined the flow of conversation with a strict adherence to traditional verse forms. He painted a semi-autobiographical picture of himself in his poem 'Totò Merùmeni'. What sounds like an Italian man's name is in fact a garbled version of *Heautontimoroumenos*, title of a comedy by the second-century-BC Latin playwright Terence and meaning in ancient Greek 'the self-punisher' – a reminder of Gozzano's awareness of previous writers. The poem begins (all Gozzano translations in this article are by Nichols unless otherwise stated) with a description of the villa where the twenty-five-year-old Totò lives with his sick mother, white-haired great aunt and mad uncle:

With its untended garden, its spacious rooms, and its fine seventeenth-century balconies alive with verdure, the villa appears to be taken from certain verses of mine, a model villa almost, out of a children's reader [...]

Time to visit Guido's own villa, and I drive up to Agliè. This really is Piedmont, on the north-ern edge of the Po Valley plain at the foot of mountains rising towards the Mont Blanc range, beyond which lie France and the French-speak-ing part of Switzerland. Agliè proves to be more of a town than its population of 2,600 might suggest. It contains a spectacular 300-room

palace, whose present incarnation dates from the seventeenth century and which was once a residence of Italy's former ruling house of Savoy. Il Meleto, whose grounds still include the apple trees that gave it its name, is nearby, surrounded by maize fields basking in the summer heat.

I meet Renzo, the soft-spoken, silver-haired cus-todian who lives in a small house beside the villa. He's expecting me, waives the normal five-euro entrance fee and shows me round. Il Meleto was remodelled by Guido in 1904 in the Liberty style, containing among other things a beautiful art nouveau stained glass window. I observe that I am the only visitor, although the museum is open to the public, on this sunny Saturday morning in July. 'Lots of people don't know the villa is here,' Renzo admits. 'It's not much advertised.' He has a slightly different version of the demise of the Gozzano family, saying Erina's two daughters stayed in Italy but both died childless. He adds that, after the Gozzanos, almost all the contents were sold locally, only a writing desk remaining. But the Conrieris later managed to find and buy back ninety percent of the former possessions, returning them to the villa. In one well known poem, 'The Friend of Grandmother Speranza', evoking the Italy of two generations earlier, Guido penned a much quoted phrase – 'good things in the worst of taste' – to describe the interior of the house he has in mind. You could say the same about the *objets d'art* that fill Il Meleto now, with its chinoiserie, oil paintings and decorated ceilings. But it would be a little unkind. I notice a doll beside the bed in Guido's room. 'He played with dolls when he was a child,' Renzo says. 'And, you know, when he visited the East he travelled with another man.' Renzo smiles sadly and we move on into another room. For two men to journey together to Asia in 1912 (the unrealised hope was that the cruise to India and Ceylon, now Sri Lanka, might improve his health) scarcely seems proof of anything, but I decide to look into the matter further in due course.

Lilita encourages me to return to Il Meleto in September, when the 2015 Gozzano awards will be made. I promise I will and when I talk vaguely of booking a hotel in the area for myself and my wife she makes us the irresistible offer of staying in the villa itself, whose attic floor she has turned into an apartment.

Meanwhile, something happens to rekindle my interest in Gozzano's religious beliefs (or lack of them). I am aware that for all his talk of being an atheist he was intrigued by medieval saints and mystics and, not long before he died, wrote a screenplay for a film, never made, about St Francis. I also know that, as he lay dying in Turin, he was visited by Mario Dogliotti, once a less than godly student friend and companion on nocturnal escapades but who had an unexpected religious conversion, becoming a Benedictine friar. Not thinking about Gozzano, I happen to visit an early book exhibition at a Benedictine abbey east of Rome in Subiaco (a town better known as the birthplace of Lucrezia Borgia and film-star Gina Lollobrigida). I realise that it was here that Dogliotti lived and in the gift shop I find a book of his letters, published by the abbey itself in 1971 and entitled *My Road*. Most of them are to relatives but one, written shortly after Guido's death, is to Silvia Zanardini, a friend of the poet's family. In 1916 Dogliotti spent six months at the war front but, after being sent back to Subiaco on health grounds, stopped off in Turin on the way and was called to Guido's bedside. In a visit on 16 July, he says, what began as chat between old friends 'soon, rising imperceptibly in tone, reached the point where both of us were secretly heading. From that moment we must consider that God was present: from that bed, as from an altar, I raised to Him that heart renewed in the name of Christ [...]' The book's anonymous editor quotes 'confidences gathered from the Gozzano and Dogliotti families' to assert that Guido gave confession to his friend on 17 July. He died just over three weeks later.

Tantalising if not, perhaps, totally conclusive. There are unanswered questions, also, about Guido's love life which might not merit such attention were it not that so much has been written about his affair, if that is what it was, with fellow poet Amalia Guglielminetti, his fascinating correspondence with her, his alleged dalliances with other women, and the role that love's misfortunes play in his poems.

From photographs taken before tuberculosis took hold, Guido appears as a good-looking, slightly-built young man. A female friend, Carola Prosperi, wrote: 'Of medium height, with authentic gold-blonde hair, a body of elegant thinness, pale face, somewhat gaunt with pronounced but regular features, weak blue eyes behind the lenses of his *pince-nez*, he was not exactly beautiful but was distinction in person.' Women, we gather, found him attractive. Which brings us to Amalia.

She was two years Guido's senior. They met in 1907, the year his illness was diagnosed, at the Culture Society, Turin's premier arts association. A scathing account of their relationship appears in the standard biography of the poet by Giorgio De Rienzo, uncharitably titled *Guido Gozzano: Short Life of a Respectable Liar* (1982). Soon after the first encounter, an intense correspondence begins in which the evidently smitten Amalia, perhaps misled by his fulsome praise for her new poetry book, *The Foolish Virgins*, is pushing forward and Guido, almost from the outset, is pulling back, concerned the involvement could go (and later apparently *did* go) further than he is ready for. More than a century later, the letters are still hard to read. Guido laments Amalia's *bellezza* ('a terrible enemy to the seriousness of our friendship') and ungallantly rues the imprint, during one close encounter, of her 'canines' (the same image occurs later in his poem 'A Woman Reborn'). She responds in patient, if pained, fashion to his hurtful rebuffs of her advances. Their on-again, off-again relationship culminates in early March 1908 when they have what De Rienzo calls 'a meeting as lovers'. Guido instantly regrets it. In a letter that De Rienzo calls 'a masterpiece of cruelty', he says: 'I have never loved you [...] [W]ith you, who are the most elect feminine spirit whom I have ever met, and with you who say that you love me,

I have always been and wish to go on being frank: I do not love you. And the most honest decision on my part is that we should separate.' This, too, ends up being versified, in 'The Frank Refusal':

I cannot love, and I have never loved
ever! [...]
So don't direct your little snow-white feet
to the dark soul of one who holds his peace!

And yet, remarkably, they did go on being friends, albeit on Guido's terms, continuing to correspond and to meet. The last photograph I have seen of the two of them together dates from August 1914, the month the First World War broke out (Guido, of course, was found unfit to serve). It shows them lounging against a railing on an esplanade on the Italian Riviera, Guido holding a parasol. Illness has taken its toll on him, he looks emaciated. Amalia remains a flashing-eyed Italian beauty. After Guido's death she had a short affair with the writer Dino Segre, also known as Pitigrilli, whose 1921 novel *Cocaine* was republished in English three years ago. She was to die, aged sixty, of complications from a fall while rushing to a bomb shelter during an Allied air raid on Turin in 1941.

Guido's poems and prose also contain references to tumbles with housemaids and peasant girls, who are imagined as less hard work than educated upper-middle-class women. For example, from 'Eulogy of Ancillary Amours':

Like figures out of the *Decameron*,
maidservants give us, and without torment,
more healthy pleasure than the mistress can.

Gozzano's *alter ego* Totò Merùmeni, after dreams of actresses and princesses, also settles for an eighteen-year-old cook:

While all the house is asleep, that girl, her feet quite bare,
fresh as a ripened plum in the coldness of daybreak,
comes to his room, kisses his mouth, and then and there
leaps onto him in bed, flat on his blessèd back.

In one of his most celebrated poems, 'Signorina Felicita', Gozzano's poetic persona holds out to an 'almost ugly' country wench suggestions of matrimony that both of them know is not going to happen:

You never think of Nietzsche...
I could be happier with such a creature
than with some whining intellectual [...]

How literally to take any of this? We need to recall that the theme is a literary commonplace going back at least to Horace. As for Signorina Felicita, commentators note that Félicité is the name of the servant girl at the centre of Gustave Flaubert's 1877 story *Un Coeur Simple*.

At the same time as he was skirmishing with Amalia over their relationship, Gozzano was also writing letters of a rather different kind to his fellow poet and close friend Carlo Vallini. These are Exhibit A in De Rienzo's claim that there is evidence for 'an unpublicised gay Guido'. To check it out, I scan through the letters and find this (not included in Nichols's selection) from August 1907. It begins by addressing Vallini with the endearment '*Colomba*' (literally 'Dove'), before continuing: 'Here I am at your feet, dear heart, not to give you a blow-job – I couldn't because I've got an inhalation mask – but to tell you that things are going better [...]' Hmm. Just camp boys-will-be-boys ribaldry, or something more? (Don't worry too much about that inhalation mask, by the way – it was simply to enable him to breathe in essences considered beneficial to his lungs; he was to live another nine years). Other letters to Vallini contain similar insinuations. But what does it all add up to? Let's ignore Guido's remark to Amalia, 'It's a pity you aren't a man.' And we may put down to his inept-itude at relationships his 'fantastic project' (De Rienzo's term) to fix up Amalia in 1908 with Vallini, instead of himself, as a lover (nothing came of that). Before we are too harsh on Guido, we might remember that this was a man who knew from his early twenties that he was almost certainly doomed to a premature death, once described by him as 'the lady clothed in nothing and without form'.

The Gozzano Awards take place on a sunlit late summer afternoon in the garden of Il Meleto. Along the path through the apple orchard beyond is an installation, consisting of a mannequin dressed in a woman's costume of a century ago and poems from various countries attached to bushes with clothes pegs, all intended as a contribution to the U.N. International Day of Peace (21 September). Four actors read a selection of Gozzano's works including a particularly good reading of the poem 'Cocotte', describing how at the age of four Guido, on holiday with his family in a rented seaside villa, is engaged in conversation in the garden by a strange woman who, his mother later tells him, is a '*cattiva signorina*' (bad young lady). Then the awards are handed out. As a native English-speaker and 'the correspondent of *PN Review*', I'm asked to recite the winning entry in the foreign section, written in English by the British-born Israeli poet Ruth Fogelman, who's not present. There's also talk, involving the mayor of Agliè, about how to mark the Gozzano centenary. It's agreed it's important to try to interest the government in it, but when I check back a few months later, the planned celebrations, including conferences, exhibitions and publication of a new book by Lilita and others, still seem confined to the region.

We wake up the following morning in our attic room in Il Meleto and recall that it was here that Guido wrote poetry and was visited by Amalia. Lilita arrives and makes coffee, and we sit look-ing out over the countryside on another fine morning. I ask her hesitantly what she thinks about Guido's sexuality. 'I don't know,' she says. 'It seems the relationship with Amalia wasn't entirely platonic. But people didn't write confes-sional things in those days.' And his last-minute embrace of Christianity? 'I don't know,' she says again, noting that someone on the point of death might conform to tradition. Later, I send her the Dogliotti letter, which she hadn't seen.

Guido died, fittingly enough at twilight, on a sultry August evening in 1916. Outside, crowds were celebrating the capture of Gorizia, on what is now the border with Slovenia, from the Aus-tro-Hungarians – an event that also overwhelmed the poet's death notice in the next day's news-papers. As he expired, he looked, his mother Diodata said, 'like a Christ in ivory'.

Hair

Elaine Feinstein

How can I reassure my dismayed self in the mirror
as a hank of hair comes away in the comb?
The stuff is soft and pale, as if from a days-old baby,
and the shorn face looking back from the glass
reminds me of those bewildered French women
with scalps exposed and features suddenly huge

whose heads were shaved for sleeping with German soldiers.
My hair loss is only the common response
to chemicals which enter the blood searching out
cancer cells which have escaped surgery.
Nothing hurts. I don't feel ill. I simply sit
here, in my white pod, listening for beeps.

With what insensate vanity did I once give my age
with such precision as the years went by
as if to invite astonishment? Dunbar had Pride
lead in his 'Dance of the Seven Deadly Sins'
with wild demeanour – bonnet on one side –
I must be one of her progeny.

Once I was a witch on a bicycle with two small boys
late for school, holding on to me tightly,
my tangled hair trailing behind as I pedalled.
Did I know I was happy then?
I was young at least, and commuting a hundred miles
daily – though still behind with the mortgage.

And we loved the huge house we couldn't afford, the raspberry
brambles and wild roses in the garden,
our library where my first poems took shape –
the terracotta ceiling and sanded floor, where
young poets often came to sprawl and talk of their
messy lives, and the erotic charge

of American poetry, or hearing Jeremy Prynne,
as he paced the floor, allowing us all to share
Aristeas' vision of nomadic tribes and their purity
we all believed in – at least as he spoke of it...
Less innocent intoxications: London days,
floating in wanton drift away from home,

listening at *Better Books* or drinking in pubs
on Charing Cross Road with Andrew Crozier,
– beautiful boy, and effortless lyric poet – the litter
of whose lines aroused my own.
Long gone those days. And now, my bushy hair.
I must buy a woolly hat against the cold

or a glamorous wig from Notting Hill. Once there,
I stare through the glass window at shelves
of plaster dollies with tiny features, each face
as splendidly null as Tennyson's Maud.
Even before entering, I hate them all. I refuse
to think beyond the months of treatment to come.

A curly white fur now covers my head. Some like it.
I'm not sure, though I've junked the wig,
and today coming back from the hospital in sunshine
through Regent's Park, I watched
the branches of bare trees catch November gold
and was suffused with extravagant happiness.

Fourteen Sonnets

SAM QUILL

I

Somewhere within the second kiss or first,
affronted by her flesh, so unlike mine,
the solipsist or child in me confessed
a truth: there is a ghost in the machine.

Seeing her now, one last time in her bed,
her limbs made hard in this audacious light,
I cannot be more certain: in that head
there is a world I cannot put to right.

Unspeakable, though willing still to speak;
untouchable, though able still to touch;
she kept her heart, all other things she broke,

then took her flesh: to prove I'd met my match.
Each night in each new darkness I must wake
to meet that ghost again: *too much, too much.*

II

Affronted by her flesh, so unlike mine,
(this even in the midmost of the fuck)
as if some casual flaw in the design
of me or her, meant neither could have truck

with the one flesh, but which of us was faulty?
As if she were a sister, or a dog.
Since I knew nothing else, I tried my fealty
to my own flesh, not hers; no dialogue;

(theology, perhaps, our only hope:)
the mind can sympathise; the body, less.
But, Sister, here's the trick, here's our escape:

lie far enough away to see my eyes,
press your whole heart against my fingertip,
then humble me with your more human corpse.

III

The solipsist or child in me confessed,
or doctored his confession, or succumbed.
All this, all that is light, could not consist
in what is light alone but always seemed

obliquely anchored, seemed more to possess
a principle of weight and unity.
There's new support for my hypothesis:
when science took the measure of gravity

it found that all we see, if it's alone,
is not enough to hold the place together.
Dark matter makes the best part of the Sun.

All this, knowing the dead weight of a feather
could break the scale on which we read our own
dead weight, and so are conscious of each other.

IV

A truth: there is a ghost in the machine.
You will not see the face of your attacker,
nor meet the one who taps your mobile phone;
nor thin her blood, nor coax her vow, with liquor –

you know her only as you know a ghost.
Though you could be no closer, no more naked,
almost all is almost always lost,
and we exhaust the duties of the wicked.

If you seek her, know this: there is a stress
expressive upon every human mind,
but she will only speak under duress,

and only when the deal is double-blind;
effacing eyes, tongue, lips, all but the kiss
that names her, and is quieter than the wind.

V

Seeing her now, one last time in her bed;
the engine cuts, then silence: and we drop.
Would this be any different were she dead?
A body, once in motion, does not stop;

only an equal and opposing force
(in Newton's law this holds a certain truth)
can brace a falling body in its course:
a lever big enough will move the earth.

But we cannot be equal, and we fall;
unequaled, unopposed, are falling through
a deeper, always emptier night, until

one tick before the whole clock's wound up new:
then everything that is, is cold and still.
Sometimes a way of putting it will do.

VI

Her limbs made hard in this audacious light
appear to curl such space on their inverse
that but to prick her with a needle might
through that bright fissure drain the universe

or make her bleed till all we knew was blood
and she and I suspended in the flood.
But lines like these destroy a poem's health.
Its half-life gone and this its dying breath.

[   ]
[   ]
[   ]

[   ]
[   ]
[   ]

VII

I cannot be more certain: in that head,
lithe in its spate of youth and erudition,
there is no counter-tide to stem the bleed
of thought, that, in somatic transposition,

articulates in flesh her mindful charge,
and moves us in our mutual element.
(If Stow had made his *Tempest* for the stage
you'd think that words were to its detriment;

but, mercifully, that film's too young for sound.
Those lovers cannot speak, and so each sings
the name repeated in each audient mind,

against the tyranny of silent things.)
I hear her speak: *and by that sleight of hand,*
who hears not Yahweh, when she speaks in tongues?

VIII

There is a world I cannot put to right:
Who lies beside us, in your coupled arms?
I counted two when we put out the light,
but who has come among us in your dreams?

There is always another, and another;
we bear each other up, we make a chain.
What keeps us here is that enduring tether;
we find what we will always want again.

And since this is forever, we'll run dry
of pillow talk, pet name, and solemn vow;
so I must see her eye within your eye,

and you must bear up those who need you now
as now I need you: without them, we die.
What's that beneath you, in the undertow?

IX

Unspeakable, though willing still to speak
between the sonar's pulses; in the fizz
and butchery of qualia; the leak
of knowledge we swore never to disclose;

in each redacted word or censored line:
you ask me why I will not give it up.
That faculty which would make blood from wine
gives answer from the bottom of the cup.

It says: Your poem cannot make a plea
for life to sign its contract; its occasion
is always what is always yet to be;

we have no heart for menace or coercion.
I ask you: By what cruel telemetry
do you now call these verses into motion?

X

Untouchable, though able still to touch;
the way two stars, some thousand lightyears distant,
when they align will lean across the breach
and seem one light; so we, seen from the constant

loving eye and aleph-point of vision,
appear one body still, seem still to be
fixed and eternal: one ecstatic neuron,
burning in the skull of Ptolemy!

Between when I first wrote those words and when
you'll read them (so that's now) the sky will sift
its pan of gold, and from the rubble spin

itself out of itself, till all that's left
of our twin stars is dust. *And from my pen
your faulting voice will cut itself adrift.*

XI

She kept her heart, all other things she broke
asunder, to their atoms, or the thought
which thinks those atoms, or to the mistake
by which the thought conceives her separate heart.

*(Gently, obliquely, we police our errors;
until, made whole, then double, we distinguish
two lives: the one that thinks, and that which matters,
each with its rites and temples, and its anguish*

at what it might have been.) But she kept hers;
and keeping that, does she not keep the time
that only hearts can mark; that does not err

or stutter, in our multiversal rhyme
of thing with thing? Or its obtuse obverse:
the private breath. She took my little dream,

XII

then took her flesh, to prove I'd met my match
in all that now remains. *Her light was out
and while I slept she must have made the switch:
her changeling flesh for every vital blot*

*in this bright world, and its dark paramour
in vital thought. We answer to her name,
and live under the freedom of her law;
life's burn is hers, and its sustaining flame.*

*(Now think only of dawn's simplicity.
Think only now of light, and of the sense
of lightening through closed lids, in memory.*

*Think of the birth of light; its vigilance
in tempering the vulnerability
of tired eyes, its soft omnipotence.)*

XIII

Each night in each new darkness I will wake
to test how far the light is in abeyance.
Theology was succour in a funk
and to that love I offer my resistance

not as the gun but as its metal does,
a more or less conducting element.
In verbal disambiguation is
the hard elenchus, through which our ferment

is spoiled to wine. Still keener, to refine
her living ghost to its more piquant will;
so to divine what in us is divine;

is all I ask of verses, and is all.
(The labour's nearly done at this machine
on which I write: *I'm finished with this quill.*)

XIV

To meet that ghost again: *too much, too much.*
But I have said too much for that conceit;
whatever ghost there is now stares with such
unanswerable force, I cannot meet

her eyes to make a poem of it. *The wind
has rushed the town, the weather is deciding
that the weapon must outlive the wound;
we hear enough to hear the song subsiding.*

*The big receiver tilts one more degree
towards the source, then settles at its rest
to sing again, an altered frequency.*

Her ghost has been committed, we adjust
the lights, and find ourselves in company,
somewhere within the second kiss or first.

The Quarrel with Ourselves
Poetry and Criticism

• The PN Review Lecture: Oxford, 27 November 2015 •

I WANT TO CONSIDER one fairly well-known statement about poetry, and about the way we talk about things including poetry. Many will recognise its author as being W. B. Yeats:

We make out of the quarrel with others, rhetoric, but of the quarrel with ourselves, poetry. Unlike the rhetoricians, who get a confident voice from remembering the crowd they have won or may win, we sing amid our uncertainty; and, smitten even in the presence of the most high beauty by the knowledge of our solitude, our rhythm shudders.

I have no idea how often the first sentence of this has been quoted over the years, but the figure must be a high one. Naturally, it has been quoted apart from its context – but pointing this out should not be taken for some game-winning production of the critical ace ('If you read on, I think you'll find that what he *really* means is this, and not what you are saying at all'). Yeats's remarks come from his short prose book *Per Amica Silentia Lunae*, written in 1917 and published simultaneously in London and New York on 18th January, 1918. To translate those dates into the author's age, the work was written when Yeats was fifty-one, and published when he was fifty-two years old. He had been publishing poetry since he was nineteen years of age, and critical prose since he was twenty-one, so his statement here has a good deal of time and experience behind it. Yeats by this time knew a few things, that is to say, about both poetry and quarrelling.

Definitions of poetry are not very helpful things – at least, they are not at all helpful for the making of poetry. It will not help a poet to do a good job if she or he prepares to welcome the Muse by reciting the mantras that poetry is at bottom a criticism of life, or that poets are the unacknowledged legislators of the world. The reason for this is that any definition we care to provide is by its nature a nugget of critical thought and expression, and this goes for those pieces of critical theory masquerading as verse, such as the dogma that 'a poem should not mean | but be', or many of the grander pronouncements in the poems of, say, Wallace Stevens. Wheelbarrows and plums, too, have been critically wheeled out and savoured, perhaps too much. Thinking we know what poetry is does not give us a way to write a poem; or, to commit the contemporary critical sin of value-judgement, it does not guarantee a good poem. None of this is to deny that it is the business of critics to say (and if they're lucky, to say memorably) what they think poetry is: implicitly, all worthwhile poetry criticism does this, however incrementally or subtly. But between critical thought, and the ways in which the mechanisms of an achieved poem can be said to enact a kind of 'thought', there is a real and well-nigh insuperable distinction.

Distinctions can be 'blurred', of course; but a blurred distinction is simply one that is rendered unclear, not one that has been abolished. Criticism, like poetry, ought to be in the business of clarity: good criticism makes clear what was otherwise indistinct, while a good poem puts something hitherto not merely indistinct but entirely non-existent into its own unique clarity of existence. Criticism necessarily talks in terms of things we know about, in however intellectually demanding a way; a really new poem, on the other hand, is something we never knew before, and which we had no means of imagining.

Put like this, it might be difficult to see where any difficulties could possibly arise. Poems are poems, and criticism is criticism, and all is well. And yet, as Yeats and others in other times have known, the world is not like this, for both poetry and criticism have inherent tendencies to know what is best for each other. At its worst, this can result in the kind of poetry that disdains all possible readers in the name of its own unchallengeable authenticity, demanding only a criticism that has already passed the test of appreciating it, and the sort of criticism which knows in advance what does and does not make a good poem, then proceeds to assess poets and subjects in accordance with standards it insists upon as normative.

Not that Yeats, you will notice, says anything about 'criticism'. Instead, he mentions 'the quarrel with others'; and this goes further than mere disagreement on literary judgements. What is a quarrel? The OED offers two definitions which seem to cover Yeats's intended ground. It is 3.a. which first occurs to us, perhaps: 'A dispute or argument; a violent contention or altercation *with* another person, or *between* persons; a disruption of friendly relations.' This itself spans a good deal, for a 'disruption of friendly relations' is one thing, and a 'violent contention' quite another. There is also sense 2.a. to consider: 'A ground or occasion of complaint *with* (also *against*, †*to*) a person, leading to hostile feeling, words, or action; a reason for having, or cause of, unfriendly or unfavourable feelings towards another person; a state or feeling of hostility resulting from any such cause. In recent use influenced by sense 3a and used esp. in negative contexts, freq. as object of *to have*.' This catches a lot of what 'the quarrel with others' might mean, but how far does any of it answer to what Yeats calls 'the quarrel with ourselves'?

It may be that the word here straddles two quite different kinds of disagreement, or two distinct fields of combative engagement. But the main force of Yeats's use of 'quarrel' is one of surprise: surprise that a word from the aggressive contentions of a public arena should be applied to something as apparently inward-looking as poetry, and to something as seemingly private as the self. Inclined as Yeats may have been to view himself later as one of 'the last Romantics', there is little that is conventionally romantic about this: the feel of Wordsworth's definition of poetry, as 'emotion recollected in tranquillity' is far from the kind of turmoil envisaged here. It's far, too, from what passes for the truth now, almost a century after Yeats made his formulation. So much so, that it is entirely plausible in contemporary poetic and critical culture to replace 'quarrel' with 'agreement': nowadays, we make out of the agreement with others, rhetoric, but of the agreement with ourselves, poetry.

Most of what I want to say at present concerns poetry; but that will have to be said in the medium of critical prose – of 'rhetoric', if you like; and so it may be useful to cast a glance at the kind of writing that concerns itself critically with poetry. Here, agreement is a common currency: not only is there an underlying consensus about fundamental things, but even a consensus about the positive value of consensus itself. Partly, this can be accounted for by the enormous changes which affected critical discussion in the twentieth century, the most significant of these being the emergence of professional academic criticism, that vast acreage of words published to be consumed in passing by a few assessors and dispensers of patronage, and destined to lose even this tiny audience in a short time. Here, while there may be a hundred methods of jockeying for position, along with the wholly honourable presentation of genuinely new information, there is really little room for any thoroughgoing rejection of what is taken for granted by those who have themselves the power to grant things. Any powerful consensus does not feel the need to formulate itself; and the more powerful it is, the less need there will be.

Perhaps, even so, the dimensions of a consensus in contemporary criticism may be estimated with reference to what is now plainly beyond the pale. Take, for example, T.S. Eliot's definition of criticism, made in 1923, as 'roughly speaking, the elucidation of works of art and the correction of taste'. One test of this in our contemporary conditions would be to ask whether it would, or would not, be regarded as fit to publish in an academic context: the red pencils of how many peer-reviewers would hover over it, ready to strike? The statement in itself would be seen generally as objectionable, because too clearly spoiling for a fight, and the key terms would be exposed as either false or out of date. In the large field of endeavour that now identifies itself as 'humanities', for instance, an unselfconscious belief in things called 'works of art' would be understood as a sign of (at best) under-educated naiveté; 'elucidation' would be marked down as something epistemologically far too sure of itself, and 'taste' identified as a category insufficiently historicised or theorised; while any notion of 'correction' would be enough

to consign the piece to the netherworld of outright rejection. Who, it might be asked (appealing implicitly to the consensus of upright fellow members of the guild) does the author of such remarks think he is? And that question, too, can be supplied with rhetorical answers – answers, in other words, that know themselves to be safe from further questioning: he is an elitist, a cultural conservative, and a dead white male. Defend those things (it is generally understood) only if you dare.

Actually, the T.S. Eliot of 1923 was trying to stir things up, and hoping for a productive degree of unacceptability, even then. And his essay, which bore the archly neo-Arnoldian title of 'The Function of Criticism', affected to disdain the ruck of raised and squabbling voices, floating above them like a sublimely untroubled hot-air balloon:

But on giving the matter a little attention, we perceive that criticism, far from being a simple and orderly field of beneficent activity, from which impostors can be readily ejected, is no better than a Sunday park of contending and contentious orators, who have not even arrived at the articulation of their differences. Here, one would suppose, was a place for quiet co-operative labour. The critic, one would suppose, if he is to justify his existence, should endeavour to discipline his personal prejudices and cranks – tares to which we are all subject – and compose his differences with as many of his fellows as possible, in the common pursuit of true judgment. When we find that quite the contrary prevails, we begin to suspect that the critic owes his livelihood to the violence and extremity of his opposition to other critics, or else to some trifling oddities of his own with which he contrives to season the opinions which men already hold, and which out of vanity or sloth they prefer to maintain. We are tempted to expel the lot.

No vulgar quarrelling here, Eliot seems to protest, in this atmosphere so pointedly distinct from any 'violence and extremity'. And yet the entire passage is, while acute and witty, also at least abrasive if not downright rude; in tone, it is nothing if not quarrelsome. Somehow, what claims to be an appeal *for* consensus is pitched emphatically *against* the conditions of consensual discussion.

Avoiding arguments is, of course, another defining characteristic of the presently dominant consensus, when it comes to things like the criticism of poetry. Obviously, critical discussion itself displays a good deal of plurality, and a degree of partiality: particular poets have particular followings, and patterns of appreciation (like patterns of neglect) are multiple. It is even possible to put in print one's failure to appreciate a poet whom others appreciate warmly (though there are certain – quite strict – bounds of propriety to be observed in this). At the same time, the consensus about how we can discuss poetry, and how we ought to discuss it, is observable and strong. In this, there are two principal, and complementary, patterns of behaviour. The first is a commitment to praise: to positive value judgements wherever possible – and indeed, even wherever challenging. In this respect, the ideal is to be as near as achievable an indiscriminately positive appreciator of poets. The second is to meet any difficult and non-consensual arguments with silence: knowing whom not to engage with is just as important as knowing whom to praise. These rules apply most obviously to the critical discussion in and around the 'poetry world', but they apply also (differently inflected) to the realm of academic discourse. Here, too, quarrels need to be avoided like the plague. One potent means of quarrel-avoidance is plurality itself: where there is room for everybody, no one is going to argue about the shape of the room. In place of unrelentingly positive evaluation on the part of poetry reviewers, in academe there is whole-heartedly passive receptiveness to those other academic writers judged to be the current key players in the discipline, who must be honoured by regular citation, and whose areas of interest must be accepted without question as being important. Those areas are not all necessarily literary by any means (though the academic currency of particular authors does fluctuate, and has to be watched attentively); many are broadly historical, cultural, and political. In relation to these, no young academic can afford to question current market valuations, nor is she or he in the slightest to be blamed for their needful caution. Yet the effect over time is a baleful one, for the possibility of proper critical discussion within the forum of specifically academic and professional discourse becomes more and more constrained, to the point at which it may disappear altogether.

Concentration (and constraint) have been going on for a long time. The contemporary academy, and the fearsomely huge body of published contemporary poets, are closely allied, sometimes to the point of wholesale identity. But where we now have a relationship of mutual esteem between poets and their critics (or, more accurately in a lot of cases, between poet-critics and critic-poets who frequently co-exist in the same person), there was once wariness and a measure of real distrust. In 1963, Elizabeth Bishop could write to Robert Lowell about a recently published critical symposium on his poem 'Skunk Hour', registering the unwelcome effects of the then-dominant models of critical attention to poetry on display:

Oh dear I do loathe explanations, explanations, etc. – and it seems to me a 'symposium' should do more, or less, - something quite different, at any rate. All this explaining shd. mostly go without saying, I think – and yet that is what people ask for. [...] To hell with explainers – that's really why I don't want to teach.

The fact that Bishop did end up having to 'teach' shouldn't lessen the force of this; indeed, it may even make that force more interesting. And her own critical powers are revealed in the same letter, with a few lines on 'Skunk Hour' that easily surpass anything written about the poem before or since: 'it has so much more *life* to it than you'd ever guess from those essays – and so much wonderful, distant, slightly-hesitant, but nevertheless sure-as-a-hymn kind of northern music to it.' Yet amid all the noise of the tenured 'explainers', the professors and the poet-critics and the critic-poets at work here, there, and everywhere in a booming university system that

makes good money from the humanities, Bishop knows exactly what is never being mentioned:

The trouble is – excuse my clichés – as people grow older, non-artists, that is, they do have to steel themselves so much, forget so much and try to pretend that everything's all right so much. They are afraid, probably rightly, that poetry – any art – if they take it hard, might upset them – so they pretend they like it while at the same time they resist it absolutely.

Fifty-two years later, this is one of those truths which remains unsayable; to air it now – whenever, say, yet another anthology makes its marketing pitch on the promise that poetry can change your life for the better – would be understood simply as quarrelsome, the work of an elitist, a spoiler, or (at best, and condescendingly) a useful gadfly. Yet it is a great poet writing to another great poet; I myself think that what Bishop says here is true. If people really understood most poetry, or understood what it takes to write most true poems, they would be shocked rather than inspired. The truth is, everything is not 'all right'; and real poetry tells this truth. Few creative writing courses, it is fair to say, have been founded on such a premise; nor does it sell many books, or make many careers.

The case is seldom made – for altogether understandable reasons nowadays of practicality and self-interest – for poetry's necessary divorce from institutional processes of knowledge and pedagogy. Yet there is a venerable quarrel between poetry and intellectual abstraction. Ironically, the quarrel itself can fuel poetry. One instance, from a thousand, is in John Keats's *Lamia*:

Do not all charms fly
At the mere touch of cold philosophy?
There was an awful rainbow once in heaven:
We know her woof, her texture: she is given
In the dull catalogue of common things.
Philosophy will clip an Angel's wings,
Conquer all mysteries by rule and line,
Empty the haunted air, and gnomèd mine –
Unweave a rainbow, as it erstwhile made
The tender-person'd Lamia melt into a shade.

This is much less grown-up than Bishop; but the fact that added intellectual maturity would ruin it is really just one way of noticing the power and authenticity of its perspective. And the narrative of *Lamia* as a whole, we should remember, is rather more circumspect on these issues. Nevertheless, 'cold Philosophy' is always ready with its wing-clippers whenever academic criticism takes stock of poetry; and just because the philosophical assumptions of Keats's time have changed, we should not assume that the imperatives of institutionalised knowledge have put those clippers away. On the one hand, plenty of powerful interests know what it is the business of poetry to be doing; on the other, reciprocally, there is no shortage of poets who look to those interests in order to learn what it is that they should do. Luckily for those concerned, there is no quarrel about this, for all sides are happy to be in underlying agreement. Yet the contemporary academy is intellectually constrained and directed to a degree that far outdoes anything prevailing in Bishop's time.

It is important to say that there are wholly beneficial consequences of academic professionalism, too many to list here. Over the last fifty years, too, the academy has been the breeding ground and practical enabler of some permanently valuable scholarly and critical contributions to the way we know and think about poetry. Its authority, also, has been used for good purposes: nothing is objectionable about a system of intellectual discipline which results, for example, in Shakespeare-deniers finding themselves shut out by respectable publishers, or the blatantly perverse among readers being driven to re-value some authors (who were probably never much valued in the first place) only to a few friends in the pub. Exclusion can be a good thing. Even so, there has been for some time a state of affairs in which whole swathes of subject-attention and critical method are either devalued or declared inappropriate to present needs, and are thus rendered off-limits. A profession needs a governing narrative to explain itself to the world, and for literary academe that narrative has become one of progress – as though critical appreciation were on a par with truly progressive kinds of knowledge, such as the sciences. But who decides what 'progress' looks like? And how can something as definite as 'progress' be a quarrel?

Professional power exercises itself by being thoroughly conflict-averse. This requires consensus, and it is of the essence that consensus need not speak its name: simply, consensus is what everyone knows without having to say so. In the contemporary academy, everyone (that is to say, everyone in positions of substantial institutional and disciplinary power) knows that literary criticism can only exist under sufferance of various kinds: it should be able to historicise itself, relate itself to another approved field of attention (political, cultural, gender-based, psychological, philosophical, and even medical), and generally prove amenable to translation into other terms than its own. Everyone knows, too, that the study of authors has progressed beyond what was once thought of as a canon; that what was formerly known and valued must now be 'interrogated', and searched for ideological goods which mostly it never possessed; and that busy stocktaking of all possible academic activity, however minor, on a given topic over the last few years counts for more than serious consideration and elucidation of work from ten, twenty, or a hundred years ago. The most polished and professional work in academic criticism is generally assumed to be that which is most up-to-date, most closely attuned to the unspoken consensus of the day, and most nearly (in intellectual terms) empty. Everybody who is anybody in academe knows all this; they do not say it, because there is never any need for them to do so. Saying it, doubtless, would simply appal them, and would be treated as a lapse in taste when, in truth, it is more in the nature of a breach in protocol. And what exactly, these days, is the difference?

In some ways, as far as literary criticism's interests are concerned, this does not greatly matter. Art may not need to bother its head with the opinions of professors in the humanities (and there are an awful lot of these in the world) for very much longer: already, almost nobody outside the academy itself is listening, and before long few will be willing to make the investment (as students, or as apprentices in the increasingly expensive and ramshackle system) in finding out. The currently cried-up 'Crisis in the Humanities' is also (to co-opt another phrase from Yeats) one of those 'catch-cries of the clown' that amounts in the long run to little more than the squealing of various interests as they vest themselves a little deeper in the shallow politics of their time. In truth, the humanities were in 'crisis' long ago – a crisis of self-belief, in fact, which was most obviously enacted in the advent of so-called 'theory' in literature departments in the 1980s – and their heart buckled and failed under the pressure of that doubt. Since then, 'theory' may have lost a good deal of its lustre, but it is true to say that the non-literary has set the terms for much of what passes as professional literary study, and by now it commands all the powers of patronage that can guarantee its complete victory. How else can it be, for instance, that projects announcing themselves as 'interdisciplinary' routinely attract special funding from those bodies whose opinion matters to university managers, as though it were somehow more advanced, more definitely progressing, than purely disciplinary study? It is, indeed, progressing somewhere; it is progressing decisively away from literary criticism. In the process, it may succeed in putting an end to various purely disciplinary areas. Perhaps this is just as well, for literary criticism's involvement with academe has never been entirely a happy one, and is in any case not of very long standing in historical terms. Great poetry was written long before there were professors to study it, and there is no reason at all to believe that it requires them in order to happen again in the future. Universities will increasingly find themselves obliged to avoid activities that are essentially disinterested ones, and the humanities, who have decided for some time that their studies could not on any account be disinterested, must expect to have their interests presented to them by those whose money pays the bills. True, many in the humanities dislike the politics of these newly imperious interests; but the essential point – that scholars were to be like Yeats's 'rhetoricians' who are motivated by 'the crowd they have won or may win' – was conceded by the academy itself emphatically, and ruthlessly, long ago.

All of this at least leaves the field clear for criticism to do its job, a job not all that different from the description of culture offered by Matthew Arnold in 1869, when he claimed that the task of his *Culture and Anarchy* was 'to recommend [culture] as the great help out of our present difficulties; culture being a pursuit of our total perfection by means of getting to know, on all the matters which most concern us, the best which has been thought and said in the world, and, through this knowledge, turning a stream of fresh and free thought upon our stock notions and habits, which we now follow staunchly but mechanically'. Once professional learning has been systematised and reduced to nothing more than a set of 'stock notions and habits', 'fresh and free' thought must make its home elsewhere.

One must not suppose, though, that 'fresh and free' thought is ever welcomed by, or accommodating to, the dominant power structures of its time. Certainly, freshness and freedom have long been lacking from the major humanities disciplines. The humanities, on both sides of the Atlantic, may be making a lot of pained noise at present; but the essence of their complaint is that they are not loved enough. It would seem never to have occurred to the most vocal mourners that their disciplines did not come into being in order that they should be loved; nor indeed that the society from whose instinctive values (including the values that attach to tradition and art) they have declared themselves so completely apart, and to which they remain in their own estimation so insistently superior, has truly no obligation to show them its affection. When what were once disciplines of thought and study conceived and practised in terms of disinterested knowledge decide that their success is measured by prestige, peers, and patronage, and that their prime task is to 'interrogate' their own past, along with the past and the present of their fostering societies, and their fundamental shared values of aesthetic, social, and civil traditions, then they have no right to be surprised when those who foot the bill tire of their interrogations, and ask some hard questions of their own.

Perhaps the lesson to be drawn from this is that quarrels need to be wisely chosen. The 'quarrel with others' that Yeats calls 'rhetoric' is not a thing from which he himself can claim to be apart; and from early until late in his writing career, he knowingly entered and instigated quarrels with a fully rhetorical commitment. But the 'quarrel with ourselves' that he identifies with poetry is not something merely quarrelsome, not just the picking of public fights. Ideally for Yeats – and we should remember that all good poetry can imagine, though no poetry can actually achieve, a state of ideal perfection – the purest quarrels are the most nearly disinterested ones, and it is these which can bring energy into the writing of verse. Just before the composition of *Per Amica Silentia Lunae*, Yeats published his poem 'On Woman', which is less praise of femininity than an aspiration towards it:

May God be praised for woman
That gives up all her mind,
A man may find in no man
A friendship of her kind
That covers all he has brought
As with her flesh and bone,
Nor quarrels with a thought
Because it is not her own.

Obviously, there are dynamics of gendered imagination at work here which it would be foolish to deny: a man is endorsing a male-originated notion of femininity. But for now, it may be worth concentrating on the opposition which is being set up in these lines between 'friendship' and 'quarrel', and the way in which this is related to what Yeats calls 'thought'. It may be that 'thought' is one

thing – the only thing perhaps – which poetry and rhetoric have as a common property; but what they do with it is entirely different. For Yeats, we need to remember, each was still a kind of 'quarrel': man's work, to return to the gendered terms of this poem.

In 1916–17, around the same time as both 'On Woman' and *Per Amica*'s composition, Yeats was attempting a prose autobiography. Here, the ability to cover thought as with flesh and bone, that quintessentially female power for Yeats, is attributed to none other than his sometime flatmate, Arthur Symons:

That night at twelve o'clock I said to Symons, who had just come in, 'Did I ever tell you about Maud Gonne?' and till two or three in the morning I spoke of my love for her. Of all the men I have known he was the best listener; he could listen as a woman listens, never meeting one's thought as a man does with a rival thought, but taking up what one said and changing [it], giving it as it were flesh and bone.

The thoughts here plainly run into the poem, whose ideal of sympathy as against quarrel finds the same metaphor of 'flesh and bone' giving its covering to 'thought'. But Yeats knows better than to think that he can find poetry in this provision of bodily form, however much it may be needed and desired. Sex is at issue here, undoubtedly; and one thing that Yeats is asking himself at this point is whether sex – even with Maud Gonne – is enough to still the quarrelsome impetus for, from, and in poetry. Though the prose memoir names Maud – 'All my old love had returned' – the poem opts instead for Solomon and the Queen of Sheba:

Though pedantry denies,
It's plain the Bible means
That Solomon grew wise
While talking with his queens,
Yet never could, although
They say he counted grass,
Count all the praises due
When Sheba was his lass,
When she the iron wrought, or
When from the smithy fire
It shuddered in the water:
Harshness of their desire
That made them stretch and yawn,
Pleasure that comes with sleep,
Shudder that made them one.

That orgasmic 'shudder', which prefigures the climactic and catastrophic 'shudder in the loins' of Yeats's later 'Leda and the Swan', is also here the shudder in water of newly-worked iron, a made thing; and *Per Amica*'s remarks on poetry retrace this uncertain border between the erotic and the fabricated with the same word: 'Unlike the rhetoricians, who get a confident voice from remembering the crowd they have won or may win, we sing amid our uncertainty; and, smitten even in the presence of the most high beauty by the knowledge of our solitude, our rhythm shudders.'

One notion which can be taken from this is the idea of made art as something which registers a deep unease, along with an unstoppable compulsion, in its very making. That is, our selves would doubtless be happier, and more fortunate generally, if not in a state of quarrelling; but art requires that quarrel which comes from the profoundest self-confrontation in the artist. And for Yeats, this means that poetry takes the heat of the known self into the coldness of the unknown, which is also the coldness of a made form. In late statements, this has a distinctly rhetorical spin, as though it were by now a brazenly self-aware quarrel with others. As, perhaps, it is; and indeed, in sentences like these from 1937, it seems to be a quarrel with *us*:

Because I need a passionate syntax for passionate subject-matter I compel myself to accept those traditional metres that have developed with the language. Ezra Pound, Turner, Lawrence, wrote admirable free verse, I could not. I would lose myself, become joyless ... all that is personal soon rots; it must be packed in ice or salt. ... If I wrote of personal love or sorrow in free verse, or in any rhythm that left it unchanged, amid all its accident, I would be full of self-contempt because of my egotism and indiscretion, and I foresee the boredom of my reader. I must choose a traditional stanza, even what I alter must seem traditional. [...] Talk to me of originality and I will turn on you with rage. I am a crowd, I am a lonely man, I am nothing. Ancient salt is best packing.

Of the many things that might be said about this, I will content myself here with just the one: Yeats is utterly at odds with much of our own received wisdom about both self and form in poetry, damning not only the poets (and critics) who believe that freedom of form equates with a desirable freedom of personal expression, but also those poets (and critics) who think that form is something simply there to be used, like an item in the toolbox. I very much doubt that Yeats would have found much of value in modern poetry's tribal identifications such as 'formalist', any more than he would have warmed to 'postmodernist' or 'experimental'. And there is a real question mark (in terms of artistic quality, if not 'career'-valency) over all poets who solicit and embrace such academically-conditioned labels. Today, many poets still think of themselves approvingly as members of a 'crowd', with politics and cultural correctness on full display; and others still announce themselves as 'lonely' men and women, with their lives and family histories (however humdrum) as all-engrossing subjects; fewer, many fewer, are serious about being 'nothing'. Only Yeats in his time, though (and only Yeats in ours) can honestly say all three: 'I am a crowd, I am a lonely man, I am nothing'.

But earlier than 1937, it was Yeats's poetry which told the truest story about the pain of a quarrel with the self – a pain which the later statements, haughty and magnificent as they are, are perhaps too rhetorical to register. It is not that the pain is somehow put into verse through the agency of form; rather, the pain is there, fierce and unbudgeable, deep inside the form itself. It is there in the sixth stanza of 'A Prayer for my Daughter' (first published in 1919), lodged in a rhyme:

May she become a flourishing hidden tree
That all her thoughts may like the linnet be,
And have no business but dispensing round
Their magnanimities of sound,
Nor but in merriment begin a chase,
Nor but in merriment a quarrel.
O may she live like some green laurel
Rooted in one dear perpetual place.

From its first publication in 1891, until its fifteenth collected outing in 1923, the first line of Yeats's early poem 'The Sorrow of Love' had spoken of 'The quarrel of the sparrows in the eaves': at first sight, the linnet in 'Prayer for my Daughter' is related to those sparrows, with both 'chase' and 'quarrel' apparently in the realm of 'merriment'. But the older Yeats knows that a 'quarrel' can go far beyond 'merriment': in 1924, 'The Sorrow of Love' began with 'The brawling of a sparrow in the eaves', keeping for 'quarrel' the deeper resonances of 'A Prayer for my Daughter'. Those resonances are partly with earlier work such as 'On Woman', but largely they sound in the rhyme: 'quarrel'\ 'laurel'. The laurel is of course one of the oldest conventional emblems of poetry, or of the condition of being a poet; and for Yeats here it has to come face to face with its rhyme in 'quarrel'. An early draft, in fact, gives this confrontation a less figurative cast: 'when eyes upon a promised face | With present faces quarrel, | O let her live like some green laurel | That's rooted in one dear, perpetual place.' Quarrels that are face to face, and are even in some ways *about* the faces we wear in the world, are the worst; and they are both apart from poetry and a part of it, just as one word and another word, in rhyme, are both detached from and attached to one another. The poet's laurel – in which Yeats unconditionally believes – is always intimate with the quarrel behind and within the poetry.

From all of this, it follows that poetry and criticism, like Yeats's poetry and rhetoric, are mutually involved and involving. If they can have a successful relation, that is not to be achieved without other, sometimes disastrous and destructive, modes of interaction: you cannot just decide that the relationship has to work, and declare that it must do so without risk. And yet, this is what much criticism – criticism in the 'literary' sphere, and not necessarily just academic writing – believes that it can achieve. Contemporary verse floats in a thin soup of indiscriminate – that is to say, undiscriminating – praise and esteem; the unspoken cultural consensus here is one which values respect above all; and to make actual discriminations between, say, good and less good poetry is held to deny verse the respect which is its due. When the difference between written texts and marketed personality is hard to make – as it generally is now – the respect to which we rightly believe ourselves entitled as people extends to the reception being accorded to our texts. But a printed text has no automatic right to respect, and all of the respect accorded to it needs to be earned. In the contemporary literary world, it is as though reviewers received new slim volumes with the same sticker on every cover, one which asks simply 'Do you know who I am?' The poetry comes, as it were, from a place of certainty and identity, an imaginative region untroubled by any quarrels it hasn't already won; and in its turn it is received without quarrel. Above all, nothing in the process should 'shudder': the success of the poetry must find a smooth match in the appreciativeness of its reception, and the issues in the poetry – issues which it is likely to be hailed as expressing, or even perhaps *using* poetry in order to express – must be ones which a dominant cultural consensus holds to be worthwhile.

We are still, in other words, a long way behind the Yeats of a century ago. In some ways, that isn't in the least surprising; and the situation is not one to be rectified by some presumptuous and short-sighted proposal that poets and critics should get their acts together, and follow his lead. 'Go thou,' as Louis MacNeice advised in this context as long ago as 1941, 'and do otherwise'; and that is still the right course to take. But poetry nevertheless has to remember how to quarrel with itself, just as criticism needs to rediscover the power to criticise: a poet's job is to make things, and a critic's task is partly to offer correction – but real making is essential, and real correction. Anything that keys itself mainly to external standards, that lives by a supposedly life-giving consensus beyond art (or at any rate, a livelihood-granting one) is not real poetry, and not real criticism. Both things, under such conditions, become passive agents of their time, and mere expressions of a *zeitgeist*, that vacuous but ravenous abstraction in which so much cultural prestige seems still to reside. Against both, we must assert the continued relevance of Yeats's 'ice and salt', and indeed the continued relevance of Yeats himself. We must not be surprised to be called quarrelsome, and worse; but at least we will not knowingly have clipped an angel's wing.

Two Poems

Liam Guilar

Waiting Broken Echoes Fading

A grey stone cutting stands as echo of the line
faded when the tracks were torn for scrap.
In the waiting room, shadows mark the time
that time has faded from the schedule of trains.
A 14:10 survives. Arriving or departing?
Outside, rain sweeps the platform,
but the echoes of our conversations
fade in corners like old men
collecting on the edges of a funeral.
By the broken station clock.
It's always two o'clock
so I'll wait, as waiting is my habit,
for the train that's coming
through the grey stone cutting
on the faded line.

A Woman's Song

after Wulf and Eadwacer *in the Exeter Book*

They will kill him if he comes here.
Wulf is on one island; I'm on another
surrounded by fens, guarded by cruel men.
In the dreary weather I wept by the hearth
imagining my Wulf's far wanderings.

Wulf, my wolf, worry and your rare visits
made me ill, not the hunger or the cold.
A bold warrior took me in his arms;
there was joy in that and it was foul.
A song, barely sung, is easily stifled,
but listen, Eadwacer, can you hear
Wulf, singing ours, in the woods.

Argus Panoptes

Eric Langley

I.

Stay a wide awake
with each of all
your hundred eyes
           amazing:
each shot rod
is just so hot
and every dazzled cone
           is blazing.

Don't let the short-sights,
those over-lookers in.

You will be gaoler;
you will be him.
You can keep me, free
from irreversible trim.

II.

Look, see, think in key:
I'm out on wing
in your gym, where
every enthralled gesture,
every turn of captivated
limb on limb and limb,
each fallen flower at my feet
(networks of
           laylock,
           lilaz,
           nilak,
little violent rhomboids all)
should still be noticed,
still be taken down,
still be ambushed,
           noted and denoted.

Curve the key
           elliptic
to tether our covert days
to your uptorn olive tree,
and turn me out,
torn forward to a future.

Just don't let back
           a green past,
a cage-glazed echo
of dirty-white flowers,

the sound of savage lilacs
           not loud or long,
the horns and motors
           burning
           ai ai
           burning
down mid-green lanes.

III.

I'm all panned-out,
crow-toed,
a rogue grown honest:
           dazed
in the prison gym,
to be tucked in
down on your M Cells,
snug tight in P Cells,
bright lit in K Cells,
           so sensitive
           so switched saccadic.

Under the carbon arcs,
Mangin mirrors and Leigh lights
– all eyes, no sight –
nobody spots
my scattered iridescence
           pluming
           in parabolas
through concertina wire,
           blooming
on each cold-crimp.

IV.

And, blind in the hot gaze
of our artificial moonlight –

           bulb-blind to the twisting lumens,
           the threaded candles,
           as each affective bright beam,
           in all its volting incandescence,
           hits our ignite-strike
           our magnet-hum
           to spill, spin, and rift,
           out adrift from our corona

in filigree in filament
in slender air –
so slender & white,
so solide & strong –

and nobody notes
this wild
this
incoherent spin.

V.

Wax-faced, hay-stuffed,
I'm still sat still
in the back
behind ballistic-glass –
that flexes
not to shatter –
drinking wine,
eating crisps,
teaching you chess,
foreplay, and harpsichord.

Make one last cast
one call
and call;
I'm just sewing postbags here
– stitching gapes and eyebores –
just doing the gaoler
doing the gaoler
in a hundred
hushed voices.

VI.

Yes, you know they'll come,
to try their luck, and leave –
so duck it
weave it.
Sharp cattle-rustlers, drivers
disguised as sheep-herds –
all so very keen
to give you one
damn good crack.

In He comes, wings buzzing,
gadding from his arras,
out from the black room,
the wind beaten crossroads,
waltzing in to set
his strict intercept –
all slick quicksilver –

buzz buzz
all head and beard and balls.

He'll try to catch us,
buzz buzz
plucked clean, right
from the drossy interim;
he aims to arrest us; prick us out;
by opening our post;
steaming open aerograms,
with searches and seizures;
scrawling our blanks;
each pocket picking;
resigned, resealed,
and undelivered.
Buss buss

Here He comes,
buss buss
excellent in all his tricks
till the cool stainless spring
rushes in the hinge.
Till *sessho-seki*, killing stone
snake-egg hag-stone hits,
cures you, clean between the eyes.

And the blood rush
stings.

The *bringer of luck.*
The *guide and guardian.*
Murderer.

VII.

My love, you best keep wide
– awake –
among their boring stories
with all your hot hundred
dazzling
open eye-balls
alert
and
all
amazing.

Roy Fisher, *The Ship's Orchestra*

Ian Pople

Even amid the heterogeneity of Fisher's poetry, *The Ship's Orchestra* first published in 1966, is unusual. The *Orchestra* occupies fifty-eight pages of prose and was first published in one of Stuart Montgomery's elegant little Fulcrum hardbacks. Its original cover is a woodcut by David Jones of Noah and his family supervising the building of the ark. The woodcut is in Jones's signature mixture of delicacy and strong lines; in the top left-hand corner of the woodcut, Noah appears to be having his ear bent by a female figure, perhaps Mrs Noah. A group of people just above Noah and Mrs N. are clearly casting sardonic glances at Noah and toasting, ironically perhaps, the bones of the hull of the Ark below them. In the top of the picture, a pair of stylised cranes flies from right to left.

Yet, that illustration has little or nothing to do with the book-length prose poem between the covers. The narrative of the poem, such as it is, features six characters, who are players in a ship's orchestra which never actually plays. The orchestra consists of two female players: Joyce, who is the drummer, Amy, the trombonist, and three male players: the unnamed narrator of the piece, who is the piano player, Dougal the bassist, and Merrett, who plays a white, plastic alto saxophone, this latter, perhaps, Fisher's nod to the avant-garde saxophonist Ornette Coleman. Towards the end, a trumpeter, Henrik, appears from the sick bay.

Fisher has stated that he got the idea for the text from Picasso's painting *Three Musicians*, about which he comments, 'there are three clown-like figures, one of whom has a black clarinet; and who is to say that there are not four musicians? The whole question about what they are, are they there, how many are there, what plans are they in, are they features of sound or of dimension, and so forth...' and there the syntax trails off. Fisher is clearly making the point that what might be the necessary aspects of the figures in the painting are up for grabs; an ambiguity which Stuart Montgomery appears to seize on in his cover blurb:

Using the same motifs over and over he paints us a picture. Simultaneously as in a cubist canvas several sides of the subject emerge at once. [...] The musicians are lost somewhere in the depths of the ship. The blackness breaks into hallucinatory retinal images, if not as a nightmare, but more in the first stage of sleep when reality merges with fantasy and slips into the world of the surreal. It is here that his acutely perceptive painter's eye and his ear for the words makes the images so real and his surreal journey so disturbing.

Montgomery's blurb seems just as nonplussed about the poem, and is filled with hedgings such as 'not as...' and 'more in the first' and the tension of 'so real' but also 'so disturbing'.

It is here in the blurb that the term 'surreal' is first attached to the project; 'surreal' being linked to 'cubist' and 'hallucinatory'. And there *are* some similarities to other, longer surreal texts. Giorgio de Chirico's *Hebdemeros* first published in 1929, contains a lone figure, Hebdomeros, who walks around the port he lives in, often digresses into metaphysical speculation, and has disciples. Another such long surreal text is Hugh Sykes-Davis's *Petron,* in which a lone figure wanders around the countryside. In Fisher's text, the ship's orchestra, itself, does not ever leave the ship, but in the confinement and claustrophobia of its environment, is sequestered away from the other passengers.

As Fisher explained to Rasula and Irwin in 1975, such sequestration and estrangement also applies to the imagining of the text:

With *The Ship's Orchestra* [...] I wanted to be writing about something I didn't know about, which was not entailed to any sort of reality and which was in fact made up of all kinds of fantastic impressions: you know it was a ship off a movie, a ship out of children's illustrations, a ship out of other people's poems, that sort of thing. And that for me is very important – to make it fairly clear that the thing that's being written is an artifact, is to do with the subjective.

So Fisher makes it clear that the text is both fantastical and subjective. And yet this 'subjective' text is, in part, a secondary by-product of the invention of others in movies, illustrations, even other people's poems. Fisher also blurs the provenance of the poem by making generalities of 'a movie', 'children', 'other people', blurrings designed to sequester the text and its contents away from that 'entailed reality'.

Fisher's other comments to Rasula and Irwin about *The Ship's Orchestra* align the poem with other parts of his writing. He sees it as, 'an elaboration of almost hallucinatory sensory effects – tactile, olfactory, visual, [...] auditory. And the book has, in fact, a fairly simple base vocabulary of colours, substances, things like grey mucus, saline tastes, things which are body tastes, body sensations, and things in the world. [...] an exploration of familiar body sensations extended through a small perceived world.' This latter has a fascinating echo in Merleau-Ponty's comment that 'perception is not born just anywhere [but] emerges in the recesses of a body'. That small, bodily-perceived world contains the sense of what 'surreal' might mean in this poem.

Breton in *Crisis of the Object* in 1936 suggests that there are 'fields of tension' created in the imagination by the reconciliation of two different images, 'the same object, however complete it may seem, reverts to an infinite series of *latent possibilities* which are not peculiar to it and therefore entail its transformation' [Breton's italics].

Such latencies are indicated early on in *The Ship's Orchestra* when Fisher writes,

The taste of the first mouthful of whisky is a thing that creaks, like straining wood, but it doesn't quite split. (107)

The bodily perception of taste is evoked here, but also a sound and a tactility; the wood is 'straining'. On one level, this is a kind of synaesthesia; on another level, Fisher is creating a simile around the taste of whisky. That strategy also shows how the body might perceive, through taste, the possibilities of whisky becoming 'like' wood. Here the poet engages with the ontological latency of the object, the scene and the self; an engagement which is, perhaps, one of the defining qualities of Fisher's poetry. In particular, Fisher brings into contemporary poetry an understanding of what 'not peculiar to it' might mean. The individual object might be empirically verifiable but also contain latent possibilities that Fisher both recognises and makes available to the reader, availing these possibilities as he reaches out to what is latent in the 'real world' as a whole.

Such recognition of latency is overtly manifest elsewhere in Fisher's early writing. In *City,* there is a marvellous passage in which a courting couple 'become' a train guard with a parcel in his hands.

It was hard to see where the girl's feet and legs were. The suspicion this aroused soon caused her hands, apparently joined behind her lover's back, to become a small brown paper parcel under the arm of a stout engine-driver who leaned, probably drunk, against the baskets, his cap so far forward as almost to conceal his face. (37)

This sense of transformation is, again, explicitly worked in Fisher's sequence from 1970, actually called 'Metamophoses'.

Part of Fisher's surrealism is his push into the abject, which Kristeva defines as 'what disturbs identity, system, order. What does not respect borders, positions, rules. The in-between, the ambiguous, the composite.' This sense of the abject has often been associated with what is excreted by the body: faeces, urine, skin and even breath; what the body pushes out of itself. Fisher himself comments, 'In language my specialization is in the pathology of soft tissues, transient and perishable substances; when it comes to bone I'm out of my element. I'll still turn to Pound for a reminder of what hardness is'; that 'grey mucus' mentioned earlier. And Fisher explicitly calls the Birmingham of *City* a city of 'by-products'. Here, the phenomenology recognises the body in, and as, the environment.

The Ship's Orchestra plays with the idea of the 'in between' in passages such as this:

Think of what all those people you see taste like and you'd go mad: all those leaping, billowing tastes through the world, like a cemetery turned suddenly into damp bedsheets with the wind under them. So the possible taste of a person is a small thing, just a flicker of salt,

putrescence, potatoes, old cardboard across the mind, behind the words, behind the manners. (108)

Here, the phenomenology seems very similar to Merleau-Ponty's. The body's recesses not only generate the perceptions; these recesses might also offer a sense of peculiar consistencies in the perceptions. These consistencies are not only of the wind and movement but also the dampness of taste; the taste of the brine, but also the abject putrescence and the potatoes. The cardboard, too, is 'old', perhaps damp. The perceptions are recessed 'behind the words, behind the manners', recessed, in effect beyond behaviour and in a part of the person which is not articulable. Perhaps that 'in betweenness' of articulation, in some ways undermines the very notion of the poem itself.

At other points in the poem, the body is evoked in ways which seem to nod towards other surrealist attitudes to the body; the famous eyeball-cutting scene in Bunuel's *Un Chien Andalou*, perhaps, 'There is one eye now, stitched open with wire' (123). In the section containing that particular sentence we have 'There is dangling in the little concrete laboratory, too, from surprised fingers. Twisted black, like monkey limb or hair set in bitumen, stuck to itself and dried, and easy to tear. Blander to taste than anyone would think; its smell of sweet banana spreads everywhere' (123). What exactly dangles in the concrete laboratory is left to us to imagine. But Fisher describes the contents of the scene so concretely that it is easy to picture even with logical details missed out.

The 'surrealism' of the text also moves into an extrapolating explosion of meanings:

Dropping from the sky and going fast, a cone of paper or some composition fibre, white tipped with red. Disappears below my low lids, behind whatever is there for it to disappear behind. Effusion of astronaut; part of the trombone mute; spiritual part of man-made cat. (116)

Fisher is the poet of the world in very fast movement; as he writes towards the beginning of his long masterpiece *A Furnace,* 'many modes / funnelling fast through one event' (53). Part of the speed of movement in the passage from the 'Orchestra' is a simple elision of grammar. None of these three 'sentences' begins with the subject. The subject of the verb 'dropping' is given in the first sentence, 'a cone of paper', but the copula 'is' is missed out, i.e. there is no 'a cone of paper *is* dropping'. The cone of paper is also elided from the beginning of the second sentence. But those elisions are coupled with a further, deliberate occlusion in 'behind whatever is there for it to disappear behind.' Fisher's use of 'whatever', here and often in *A Furnace,* far precedes its recent use by the twenty-first century, and his usage is not a shrugging repost but a pulling of the focus into a deliberate uncertainty.

That uncertainty is, in turn, exploded into the three-noun phrases which end the extract above. Is the 'cone' the narrator sees some debris from space exploration? And we have to note that Fisher wrote *The Ship's Orchestra* in 1962–63 when such travel was in its infancy. And even that might seem more likely than the cone's being 'part of the trombone mute'; thrown in some parabola by Amy the trombonist, perhaps. And where does the 'spiritual part of man-made cat' fit in?

If this were 'language' poetry, then the case might be made for Fisher's elisions and occlusions being part of a deliberate wresting of the signified from the signifier. And others, Andrew Crozier among them, have made that kind of case for some of Fisher's work. But the juxtapositions we've just seen are less about language and more about what is perceived and how it is perceived. And here, even humans have both latent and not so latent possibilities.

About five of us then, and something of an assortment. The coloration problem touches Merrett and me more lightly, in that we are, fairly decidedly, Caucasian, although I can tell already there's a need for one of us to feel Jewish at times, and we pass this role back and forth tacitly.

(Joyce) Round-shouldered; sometimes a bit damp-looking under the arms. She hasn't unpacked her kit yet. Cans. Bins. Bubs. All five of us double violin. (108)

Given that the text was written in 1962–63, is it not only interesting that Fisher brings ethnicity to the surface of the text. It is also interesting that Fisher seems to *play* with ethnicity. In the second decade of the twenty-first century, we have a tendency to evoke and contest ethnicity with a complexity that Fisher was unlikely to have envisaged, but here, his play also contests the notion of ethnicity. Ethnicity is felt to be both constitutable, i.e. 'fairly decidedly, Caucasian', but also mutual, exchangeable between the parties, even mutable. Gender is not mutable here, not in a *Some Like It Hot* way. However, Fisher foregrounds gender in ways which are unusual for its time. The ship's orchestra has a third of its members female. Joyce the drummer is not very positively described in the extract above; and her as yet unpacked drum kit is reduced to a pair of monosyllables, 'Cans. Bins.' Fisher then closes that group of monosyllables with a colloquialism for breasts.

The depiction of such latencies among the characters has drawn criticism from even Fisher's most ardent advocates. Peter Robinson has suggested that 'One limit in Fisher's work is the location of experience in shared relationships between people. The works that might seem at first most to qualify such a statement *(Interiors with Various Figures* and *The Ship's Orchestra)* only tend on closer acquaintance with their strangeness to reinforce it.' It is perhaps noticeable that Robinson sees Fisher's limits in the 'location of experience in shared relationships'. In his later work *A Furnace,* the people who appear are part of an urban, Heraclitean flux. To some extent, they are politicised; a woman in *A Furnace* appears as 'this peasant / is English, city born' with 'No imaginable / beginning to her epoch, and she's ignored its end.' (61–62). And there are other archetypal figures in *A Furnace.* In *The Ship's Orchestra*, however, gaze is rendered intimately through the eyes of the narrator. As we have seen, that gaze may seem of its time and,

in some ways, rendered deliberately anachronistic. Elsewhere, as we have also seen, Fisher can construct a compelling phenomenology in the human body's total experience of the world.

Sometimes, those things consciously meet as when the narrator describes his own situation.

Soon there will be a meal. The food will pity me. I shall pity myself. Healthy, ambulant, I am about to be fed with cozy food that tries to make up for my being far away from home, my being a great boy criminal. (116)

The body here is the passive recipient of the food which is 'cozy'. The food is put into the body which is healthy and mobile. Perhaps there are elements of the abject, too. The food the narrator needs to ingest seems to remind him of his deficiencies. That food moving from outside the body then into it performs a psychological function of which it is the agent. The food 'tries to make up' for the psychological and emotional deficiencies of the narrator, his being away from home and his self-declared 'criminality'. This latter is, in turn, self-consciously trivialised by the narrator as if patronizing himself in a kind of self-pitying self-defence.

And what of the overall trajectory of the poem, its 'story'? The piece begins with a conventional, almost novelistic description of the orchestra's 'band stand':

The Ivory Corner was only a wooden section of wall painted white, at the intersection of two passageways. To the left of it was the longer corridor; to the right at once there was the washroom door. (106)

However, even this has its cubist moments. Existence seems slightly precarious in this description. In the first sentence, the 'was' equates the Ivory Corner with 'a wooden section of wall painted white'. But the 'was's in the next sentence seem to throw the existence of the both the corridor and the washroom door into question. They were there, but aren't they there now, even in a historic present?

Little by way of sequential events happens between that beginning and the end. And Music is studiously avoided. The instruments are, for the most part, locked away. The piano is 'locked, its lid down with crates of tonic bottles stacked on it, in the scalloped pink and gold alcove. Disposal.' (118). As to the other instruments, 'They luggage us, they follow us, they squat behind us when we're not looking.' (118). Merrett's white plastic alto is 'flourished' at one point, Dougal's bass is covered and in his cabin. We know that Joyce doesn't go 'anywhere near her drums'. Amy does actually play her trombone in her cabin and performs elaborate scales, 'Some of which slowed her up a little, but it would have been an achievement even for a woman who was sober' (120). There is an old man on the boat deck, 'sitting wrapped in his rug' who, in a reference to *Some Like It Hot* perhaps, suggests that the male band members dress up as women. The band may or may not want to go back on shore but even life on land seems fatally out of kilter, 'on ground where disused vehicles are dumped, a woman has given birth to a child in a giant aeroplane tyre' (119). When they get to sea, they find the land, 'Far from land, we sail in shallows where grey cylinders and globes lie under the water, near enough for their rivets to show' (127). That description is prescient of Fisher's description in *A Furnace* of the raising of the raising of the German Grand fleet from Scapa Flow after the Second World War, 'breaking the grey surface, hulk after hulk, / huge weight of useful iron' (75). If those boats at least had scrap value as waste, then the rivets that show near the surface in *The Ship's Orchestra* seem to be both eerie presences that evoke drowned sailors and their lives and also shipping hazards.

At the end of the poem, Amy appears to be cleaning the body of Dougal the bass player with methylated spirits; people 'tread on them in passing' (123). The final image of the poem is, '[...] I look up into the bright fog of daylight. High up in it, billows of orange smoke seem to be going past.' (124).

The Ship's Orchestra has elicited mixed reviews even from Fisher's closest friends and supporters. We've seen what Peter Robinson has to say about it. Fisher's great friend and earliest promulgator, Gael Turnbull, commented, 'To date, I haven't been able to read *The Ship's Orchestra* from start to end. In fact, I have difficulty reading more than two or three pages at a time. Sometimes difficulty reading more than two or three paragraphs at a time. Difficulty reading, sense of being halted, obstructed.' Kenneth Cox senses the body analogues of this piece from a slightly more bizarre viewpoint, calling it, 'a work of such unadulterated sensation presented in sharp prose. As such it exerts an interest similar to that of the best pornography but, lacking reason and feeling, runs out before the end and resists re-reading.' And our sympathy must go out to Kenneth Cox for having sat through all that

mediocre pornography! August Kleinzahler in his review of Fisher's 2005 *Poems 1955–2005* suggests, 'The piece feels almost as though he had fallen asleep during the break between sets with a copy of Burrough's *Naked Lunch* spread across his face.' So *The Ship's Orchestra* has always been seen as a prickly piece possibly at odds with much of Fisher's other writing. I have tried to suggest, however, that there is much here which prefigures and rehearses many of Fisher's central concerns. Rather than a kind of throat-clearing, *The Ship's Orchestra* is an important indicator of what Fisher has been able achieve in his nearly six decades of writing poetry.

WORKS CITED

All quotations from *The Ship's Orchestra* taken from: *The Long and the Short of It: Poems 1995–2005* (Tarset, Northumberland: Bloodaxe Books, 2005)

Breton, A. (1936) 'Crisis of the Object' in A. Breton *Surrealism and Painting* trans Simon Watson Taylor (London: Macdonald 1972)
Cox, K. 'Roy Fisher' *Agenda* Vol. 29, Issue 4, pp 31–40. 1991
Fisher, R. *The Ship's Orchestra* (London: Fulcrum 1967)
Fisher, R. 'On Ezra Pound' in R. Fisher *An Easily Bewildered Child: Occasional Prose 1963–2013* (Exeter; Shearsman 2014)
Kleinzahler, A. 'Snarly Glitters' *London Review of Books* 28:8. 2006
Kristeva, J. *Powers of Horror: An Essay on Abjection* (New York: Columbia University Press 1982)
Merleau-Ponty, M. *The Visible and the Invisible* trans A. Lignis (Evanston, IL: Northwestern University Press 1969)
Rasula, J and Erwin, M. 'An Interview with Roy Fisher' in *Nineteen Poems and an Interview* (Pesnett, Staffordshire: Grossteste 1975)
Robinson, P. 'Keeping it Strange', *Notre Dame Review* 22 (2006) http://www3.nd.edu/~ndr/issues/ndr22/Peter%20Robinson/Robinson-review.pdf [accessed 31 October 2008]
Turnbull, G. (2000) 'An Unpublished Commentary from 1966' in eds. R. Sheppard and P. Robinson *News for the Ear: a homage to Roy Fisher* (Exeter: Stride 2000)

Two Poems

AMALI RODRIGO

Kolmanskop

I was sun-blind and listening to the sound of water
in wind, in desert sand, water in everything but

the river or the low trough where horses once drank
the sun. What survives is a tiny archipelago of wrecks,

the river an artery that bled out and out, became
an emboss of bone and I want to ask you if you truly

believe it is brave to enlist in war that is like the distant
sound of water with its cryptic messages of *a safer world*.

Thinking of you entering airspace, anonymous over sleep,
to leave trails of diamonds on the earth in one burst

of creation and your getaway mistaken for a star's blink,
can I forgive that you can't tell apart fleeing from stalking:

those beneath your bombs or prospectors straggling
across a desert to Kolmanskop driven by legends

of diamonds the size of men's hearts on riverbeds as if
the milky way was laid down on earth for the picking?

From your great height you can't see how they lope alike
mile by blistered mile, emptying of words, bearings;

some to find anyone who will save them, others disbelieving
to be only passing through, building houses, great halls

for opera now filling with wind's arias – men moving
too swiftly for the earth's slow kindling of diamonds.

All mined out, night in a ghost town is an armoured hood
with its shrapnel of stars. Soon you'll come, my wish

my safe passage to a mythic lode, I too will say nothing,
taste the fine brine of your sweat, drink every cup of sand.

Whirling Dervish

when you have the air of dervishhood inside,
you will float above the world and there abide

– Rumi

What I feel most is gravity, the way of a pebble
entering a still pool, living through its own fall

split from the ripples above as I watch
you give yourself to air all through the night

on a hospital bed, as if sung into a trance, leaving
the world to us, an echo of reed-flute, frenzy of birds,

one small foot grazing the earth, thistledown
or light from the distant polestar

through seafaring, petal fall or wood-smoke,
vague and dissolving by dawn beneath

the spin of your star-trail, a litter
of bone and an angel weeping.

Mothball Moon

CAROL MAVOR

'Having been breathed out' [Sappho]
   my mother died.

We folded her arms
      as if she were
      a fortune cookie
      with a secret paper tucked inside.

      Now she sits in a big jar on my father's
                              chest of drawers
      where inside are his perfectly folded
      sweaters
      T-shirts
      socks
      boxer
      underwear.

      I want to know if the Moon
      shines inside the black hole
      of a big conch shell
      like a mothball inside a dark
      drawer, just opened.

I remember
      that Apollo 11 astronaut
      alone in the ship
      flying solo around the dark side of
                              the Moon
      while Neil Armstrong and Buzz Aldrin
         walked its craggy surface
         and smelled its surprising smell:
         spent-gunpowder.

      'I am truly alone
      and absolutely alone
      from any known
      life – I am it,'
      he scribbled down
      while floating around the unlit Moon.

I imagine him sucked into
      Tristram Shandy's black page
      without a speck of wit
      suffering a long Book of Hours,
      unilluminated
      without a speck of gold.

But I am mistaken.
      Far past The Garden of Hesperides,

the Captain scribbled, drolly:
'Three billion plus two
      over on the other side of the Moon
      and one plus God knows what on this side.'

Far from feeling lonely or abandoned, the
                              Captain added:
   'I like the feeling!'

When I was a child,
   a story
   a hut
   a shell from the sea
   built dreams around
      that child
      that flabby, amorphous hermit [H.D.]
      within and furnished them
   full as an egg.

My house grew
   as a mollusc exudes its shell.

   I secreted my secrets.

When you hold a sea shell up to your ear
   that dull roaring sound
   is the ocean not.

It is the echo of your own blood.
   Splashing, humming, rushing, coming
   inside your ear.

You are hearing yourself.

As Narcissus saw himself in the water
   you are Echo hearing yourself in the shell.

I knock at the empty doorway
   the octopus-darkness [H.D.]
   of the big conch shell.

I press my ear to its mouth.
   I hear my own blood moving,
   through veins of red coral.

No one is home.

Three Poems

RACHEL MANN

Chaucer on Eccles New Road

Canterbury Gardens comprises a hundred stylish apartments for the modern city-dweller...

– Estate Agent's Leaflet

From between the lines – yellow, white, stained –
speak, Theseus, speak. Of the great chain of love,
kyndely enclyning. Breathe and speak, worthy knyght.

Requite, dronke Robyn, or *stynt thy clappe.*
Traffic has a language of its own:
whispers and sighs, the chime of speeding steel,

and prying's no sin. Inquire of tram tracks,
of *Goddes pryvetee,* how long it takes to lay.
Gras tyme is doon; my fodder is now forage;

A plea for peace, Oswald reve, but here's truth:
Til we be roten, kan we nat be rype.
We all become earth, but mortar and brick?

The Pardoner is a court, prefab walls,
Ycrammed ful of cloutes and of bones,
carpet and paint. Shopping malls are relics

swarmed with pilgrims. Your garden Theseus
is poison. Enclyne your roof, shelter me.
Til it be roten in mullok or in stree.

Reading Ovid on the Underground

Look, Niobe comes [...] as beautiful as anger will let her be.

Mansion House, Monument, Cannon Street, Bank,
the electric underworld: carriages of wrists,
elbows, ripe armpits. *Stand clear of the doors.*
Words curve on all the walls. *Last chance to see!*
Five Stars, A Triumph! Pin-up faces peel.
Lear stares, his girls. He waits our flattery.

No phases of the moon for us. No sun
to mark the days. It's all show: white light, glare.
At the edge of electrocution
corpse boys, corpse girls walk the tunnels
and halls: stale breath, bodies out of time,
they teach me the meaning of words:

frantic, fears, daughters, sons, tears, alone, gone.
St Pancras, Angel, Old Street, Moorgate. Bank.
St Pancras, do you ever hear our prayers?
Our prayers are escalators. *Scala*
sounds so classy, *elevating,* but handrails
are loops of black. Vinyl prayers spin on.

Covent Garden, Piccadilly, Leicester Square.
As far down as this world goes, I go down.
Staircases move up, topple out of sight,
metal waterfalls, but no one believes my tears.
It's theatre-land. Everyone a busker here.
Michelle, ma belle. Dry your tears, I seh.

East. East. All gods arise in the east.
East Acton. East Finchley. East Cote. East Ham.
Back to the source, through the burial grounds
the Navvies bored, back beyond the dead.
Heaven's the top of a stair.
Hell's a blur, hot wind, an empty platform.

The Priest Finds Eve in Piccadilly Gardens

Mamucium: breast-place, mother, Eve –
Oh bone of my flesh, flesh of my bone,
Clay and water dredged, sweet Daub Hole.

Tonight the mysteries of glaciers
spend themselves on tarmac. Ice-caps soak us.
We're the damp-arsed. Your favoured kids.

So this is what it's like to be cast out –
East of Eden, East of Salford, benched
with drunks. Beyond the wall, buses squeal.

We're in the dark and forget the garden
was an asylum once. Bright lights, fierce crowds
dance along its edge. We'd leave if we could.

Mamucium: breast-place, mother, Eve –
Clay and water. Raw bone. It's what we are.
Can you hear me, Eve? Our breath is fumes.

Three Poems

SHEENAGH PUGH

Some Rocks Remember

*I consider induced rocks to have Alzheimers. They are the rocks
that forgot where they were born and how to get home.*

– Prof. Suzanne McEnroe, Norwegian University of Sciences
and Technology, Trondheim

Some rocks remember where north was
when they were formed. The poles wander
about the world, and you can track
their paths in haematite, magnetite,
that answer no compass, because they carry
the printout of how things used to be.
Remanant, they are called; they don't change
with the times.

           The others, the less constant,
realign themselves, fall into step
with the magnetic field, reflect the now,
the new. The knowledge of where they began
is gone, or buried where they can't come at it.
Geologists name them *induced*: liken them
to minds with Alzheimers: *the rocks that forgot
where they came from and how to get home.*

But surely it is the mind familiar
with old magnetic paths whose compass fails,
who cannot find home now, for thinking
of home that was. They have their own north,
those remanants; we all do, and when
the world's north alters, there's our needle
true to the errant pole, still pointing
to Abyssinia or Van Diemen's Land.

The Winchman on Oscar Charlie

I'd like to be the winchman on Oscar Charlie,
if I weren't afraid of heights and helicopters:
lift people lightly from a pitching deck,
head through the dark to Christmas-blazing oil-rigs,
see from high up, so often I'd almost forget
to take notice, porpoises leaping, the shadows of orca.

I met his mother-in-law at a bus stop once,
the winchman. She told me his working day
you wouldn't believe, the things he'd seen and done,
when now and again she could make him talk about them,
but there was the rub. He wasn't a talking man;
he was strong, fearless, fantastic head for heights,

and he could have filled volumes with the way
he lived the world, the betweenness, sea and sky,
land, deck and platform, that rope, danger and safety,
if he knew the words that would make them happen
for the likes of us, checking our shopping lists,
wondering why the 9:20's late again.

Departure Bay

There's a bus to Departure Bay,
it leaves on the dot.
You could get there easy enough,
but better not:
what place in the world could live up
to a name like that?

As long as you never go
to Departure Bay,
it will smell of engine oil
and wood and salt spray;
and boxes and bales and crates
will be piled on the quay.

Travellers waiting to board,
that light in their eyes,
checking their tickets again,
postponing goodbyes,
wondering what they've forgotten
and whether it matters.

What if you go, and find only
a commonplace town,
thrift shops and trumpery goods,
buildings run-down,
a vague reek of burger bars
and desperation?

For this is the surest thing
about adventure:
it never happens as well
as in the future,
and the best of a journey is never
after departure.

Literary Enough?

Philip Larkin and John Heath-Stubbs in 1954

Henry King

In June 1954, Philip Larkin published, in the Leeds-based little magazine *Poetry and Audience*, a review of *A Charm Against the Toothache* by John Heath-Stubbs. This makes an interesting conjunction for two reasons. Firstly, Larkin and Heath-Stubbs had known one another at Oxford University during the War, when Heath-Stubbs was a member of the poetic clique that also included Sidney Keyes and Michael Meyer, editors of the anthology *Eight Oxford Poets*; Larkin, however, had been '[t]oo proud, too prickly, and too unsure of himself to join the élite literary set' (Motion: 45) – yet he still bore a grudge against Meyer in particular for excluding him from the anthology. After Oxford, their careers had followed the pattern established there. Heath-Stubbs had published several collections and made influential friends like T. S. Eliot, who invited him to edit (with David Wright) *The Faber Book of Twentieth Century Verse*. Larkin, meanwhile, had resorted to self-publishing his most recent collection, *XX Poems*, and his next was soon to be published by the small Hull imprint, Marvell Press. Larkin was therefore not only reviewing Heath-Stubbs's book, but re-viewing their relationship to date.

The second reason is that *Poetry and Audience* was published from the University of Leeds's Department of English Literature, where at that time Heath-Stubbs (on the recommendation of Eliot and Herbert Read) held the Gregory Fellowship in Poetry, and was Editorial Advisor to the magazine. Larkin was, as it were, on Heath-Stubbs's turf. In light of this unequal power dynamic, Larkin's review was, as his editor Anthony Thwaite puts it, 'an amazingly self-assured notice by a Nobody of a Somebody' (Larkin 2002: xii).

Any amazement now is likely to be at the fact that there was ever a time when Larkin's stock was lower than that of Heath-Stubbs: Larkin is one of the most popular and influential poets of the last century, while Heath-Stubbs languishes unread by all but a few. The reversal of their reputations may also stand for a wider shift in the poetic landscape: Heath-Stubbs, a friend of George Barker, W. S. Graham and others of what we might call the Soho school, following the description of it as their 'second university' (Heath-Stubbs 1988: 112), came to fame during the War, but afterwards gradually sank from prominence along with his associates; Larkin took a while to secure a place on the literary scene, but became one of the most famous poets of the Movement and remains the most read. How and why this shift took place may be an inexhaustible subject, but we can see an early sign of it in the issue of *Poetry and Audience* from June 21st 1954.

Although Larkin begins his review with a personal recollection, much of the backstory of their relationship is omitted. Recalling his first exposure to Heath-Stubbs' verse as an undergraduate

in 1940, Larkin describes himself as having felt 'doubly crestfallen: at [Heath-Stubbs's] serene individuality, practised scholarship and extensive and peculiar vocabulary, and at my failure to appreciate him' (2002: 158). Larkin initially approaches Heath-Stubbs as a rival, momentarily despondent at the older poet's prowess; but subsequently as an ordinary reader, who finds nothing to grip him in the *tour de force*. 'It was not that I thought his poems bad', Larkin explains;

I just could not see why they had been written. My attention, hovering over them like a mine-detector, reported no tension, no emotional pressure, and moved elsewhere. (2002: 158)

Larkin's telling simile demonstrates how hindsight had coloured his view. Although the image evokes the wartime milieu in which they first became acquainted, it is in fact anachronistic: the design of the portable mine detector was not completed until late in 1941; in 1942 it was brought into use in North Africa, speeding the progress of Allied forces and helping them to win the second battle of El Alamein. Larkin would not have had this comparison to hand on first reading Heath-Stubbs, but uses it retrospectively to cast their relationship in a bellicose form, with Larkin as the better-equipped force outmanoeuvring his opponent.

Turning to the book under review, Larkin states that 'Mr Heath-Stubbs's poetry has not changed all that much' (in contrast with his own development since *The North Ship*), and proceeds to damn much of the collection with faint praises. Though he concedes that Heath-Stubbs's 'formidable vocabulary and ability to spin a succession of precise and brilliant images' are 'dazzling', Larkin's categorisation of his 'dramatic/historical' and 'topographical/historical pieces' suggests a Polonial joke, and he pokes fun at 'some experiments in humour I beseech Mr Heath-Stubbs not to repeat', reserving genuine praise for 'a group of personal poems, wry or distressed, that speak of himself and his life and its dissatisfactions', of which he singles out 'Epitaph' as the best, 'despite the metrical hints that Captain Carpenter is sleeping there below'.

The main thrust of his criticism is directed at what he describes as Heath-Stubbs's continued adoption of 'postures so familiar [as] to have lost all emotional force or even flavour'. Heath-Stubbs writes, Larkin argues, 'apparently in the belief that traditional poetic stances can be carried off with no more support than good poetic manners', and 'that attitudes and properties successful in the past are thereby guaranteed successful indefinitely', demonstrating his point with an exhibition of concluding lines such as 'Except the unlimited, treacherous ocean of love,' 'In the heart of a poem's crystal alone can the Spring come true,' and 'The city of mud and pearls has broken another poet.'

How should we categorise the sort of 'traditional poetic stances' to which Larkin objects? In simple terms, romantic ones: he also criticises Heath-Stubbs for 'speaking of "the Muse" or "that Irish sorcerer" (W. B. Yeats)'. This would fit the widely promulgated narrative that Heath-Stubbs and others of the Soho school 'represent the kind of romanticism which the Movement was to react against' (Lucie-Smith 1970: 85). But Larkin is not simply anti-romantic. The danger of 'traditional poetic stances', in his argument, is that they delude the poet into thinking he can 'dispense with original and re-creating emotion' – the assumption being that poetry should be what Keats called 'the true voice of feeling'. Unlike the classicist, who makes poetry from acknowledged emotions, Larkin's idea of the poet is romantic insofar as he should discover and express hitherto-unrecognised ones. It is not romanticism *per se*, but romanticism as a set of fixed conventions, that Larkin repudiates.

This is borne out in the way he engages with the terms of Heath-Stubbs's poetry. Larkin repeats the word 'charm', but shifts the focus to another part of its semantic field, away from the folk-medicinal sense of the collection's title-poem (with the echo of its semantic root in 'chanting', fusing poetry and magic) towards a quotidian, social sense: thus Heath-Stubbs's 'topographical/historical pieces' are 'charming [...] – charming, but hardly more than fourth leaders'. The culmination of Larkin's criticism is his argument that, though Heath-Stubbs is often accused of being '"too literary"', his real defect is that he is 'not literary enough' to recognise the bankruptcy of his 'traditional poetic stances' – a rhetorical inversion having, Larkin submits, 'at least the *charm* of novelty' (my emphasis). It's possible to read Larkin here in Eliotic terms, as arguing that Heath-Stubbs is insufficiently traditional precisely because his work is simply new and not 'the really new' (Eliot 1960: 50). But the charm of novelty, the excitement of the unknown, is also a romantic desideratum.

The review was not Larkin's only contribution to that issue of *Poetry and Audience*. 'Poetry of Departures' would later be published in *The Less Deceived*, but its first appearance ties in closely with his review of Heath-Stubbs. Having noted 'Epitaph' as the best poem in *A Charm Against the Toothache*, it is striking to find Larkin use the same word in the first stanza of the poem:

Sometimes you hear, fifth-hand,
As epitaph:
He chucked up everything
And just cleared off,
And always the voice will sound
Certain you approve
This audacious, purifying,
Elemental move.

The poem considers the value of escapism, and the possibility of rejecting the sensible, stultifying life represented by one's 'room, / Its specially-chosen junk, / The good books, the good bed'.

The speaker clings to phrases – '*He walked out on the whole crowd*', '*Then she undid her dress*', '*Take that you bastard*' – that speak to him of moments of intense experience when ordinary social rules are suspended; but their virtue is paradoxically in enabling him 'to stay / Sober and industrious' – and indeed 'to stay', full stop. Why not give in to the impulse to leave? The speaker admits the attraction:

I'd go today,

Yes, swagger the nut-strewn roads,
Crouch in the fo'c'sle
Stubbly with goodness

– except, as he says, that he finds it somehow

      so artificial,
Such a deliberate step backwards
To create an object:
Books; china; a life
Reprehensibly perfect.

The argument in these concluding lines is hard to follow. The key, it seems, is the repetition of 'books', from the second stanza. To deliberately fashion one's life, as if writing a story, strikes the speaker as no less false than the conformism in which he is immured. The authentic life, he suggests, is not lived in deliberate imitation of others' grand gestures, but haphazardly, even if externally uneventful. The speaker is sufficiently literary to know that he cannot rely on what he finds in books; his internal romanticism is the mechanism of his outwardly classicist adherence to the common social duties. The final line compresses a complex dynamic of holding back (the radical sense of 'reprehend') from the allure of undiscovered perfection.

In contrast to the 'sober and industrious' speaker of 'Poetry of Departures', Heath-Stubbs portrays himself in 'Epitaph' (1954: 35) as having embraced a literary career and a concomitant lifestyle of 'idleness, lechery, pride and dissipation'. And though Larkin suggests that certain 'metrical hints' point a comparison with John Crowe Ransom's 'Captain Carpenter', the similarity is also thematic: Ransom's quixotic protagonist is an absurd yet heroic loser, hacked to pieces by the embodiments of temptation he confronts. Heath-Stubbs presents himself as having had all the advantages of birth and education, but being (like the Captain) a failure on many levels: a physical misfit, a failed academic, a sinner, a writer who couldn't live by his pen, whose reputation steadily declined. The principal difference is one of tone. George Szirtes has described it, with particular reference to the poem's last lines ('hoping that the Resurrection / Will not catch him unawares whenever it takes place'), as

irony at its warmest, a joke against pomposity in mock pompous language, a dismissing of everything thought to be just too too serious. A double negative working at double negative level. One is, one might say, not unamused.

Yet this double-negative structure also infects the poem with unease: the 'best judges of the Age' and 'the public' are described as 'not averse' to Heath-Stubbs's early poetry, written '[i]n a classical romantic manner which was pastoral' (a Polonial joke, as Szirtes points out, which Larkin perhaps echoes in his review), implying only qualified enjoyment – and besides, as he admits, 'his profit was not financial'. The poet may be said to have given himself to a bohemian literary life, but not without disappointments. In this, 'Epitaph' can be read as an equivalent to 'Poetry of Departures', written from the other side of the looking-glass.

It isn't surprising that Larkin appreciated 'Epitaph', being the poem closest to his own in its techniques and concerns. But to better understand the contention between these long-time rivals, we must place 'Epitaph' alongside one of the poems Larkin alludes to censoriously: 'Elegiac Stanzas (in memory of William Bell)'.

Indeed, the poems are literally placed alongside one another in A Charm Against the Toothache, and again in Heath-Stubbs's Collected Poems, where they mirror each other across the spine: both are poetic memorials composed of six rhyming quatrains, although apparently only one is in earnest. The correspondences continue: where 'Epitaph' records Heath-Stubbs's 'schooling in the University of Oxford', the elegy to Bell is footnoted 'Oxford, January 21st – 23rd, 1949'. And in the final stanza of 'Epitaph', Heath-Stubbs describes himself as 'having outlived his friends' – probably a reference to his Oxford contemporaries Drummond Allison and Sidney Keyes as well as Bell, for whom David Wright (1965: 19), in his anthology The Mid-Century, provides this biographical note:

William Bell was born in 1924 and killed climbing the Matterhorn in 1948. Like Keyes and Allison he was educated at Oxford, though not at the same time. [...] Bell's posthumous volume of poems, Mountains Beneath the Horizon, was published by Faber and edited by his friend John Heath-Stubbs.

'Elegiac Stanzas' is written in the 'classical romantic manner' Heath-Stubbs and his friends cultivated as undergraduates: for example, the allusion to Yeats to which Larkin took exception (though he might also have complained about the clanging pun in the same stanza, 'the bell's last groan'). But if its purpose is to memorialise Bell, how does this reflect on its counterpart? Is 'Epitaph' intended to memorialise Heath-Stubbs? That seems unlikely, given his irritation at its popularity: it is followed in the Collected Poems (1988: 326) by 'Epitaph Revisited (1986)' in which he describes the original as 'wretched verse' and 'sad stuff' – a joke epitaph that threatens to become a real one. Another possibility is that 'Epitaph' is a joke with a serious subtext, written rather to bury his younger self than to praise him and his early poetic style.

One reason for thinking so can be found in Heath-Stubbs's Collected Poems, where 'Elegiac Stanzas' and 'Epitaph' (and 'Epitaph Revisited') rest in the middle of the volume, despite dating from his first two writing decades. The reason for this is that Heath-Stubbs decided to arrange the contents not in chronological order, but with the poems written after his 1965 Selected Poems first and those before it in a second section, followed by appendices for translations and longer poems. The motivation for this was his sense of there being 'little written before about my fortieth year which I can now read without a certain degree of embarrassment' (1988: 21), although (echoing the fifth stanza of 'Epitaph') 'good judges praised them and respectable editors were willing to print them'. If the standard narrative is that the Movement poets like Larkin reacted against the romanticism of the poets like Heath-Stubbs who had established themselves in the 1940s, then the forties poets' own account is that by the following decade, having come through 'the university of Soho', they were already reacting against their own youthful romanticism, a reaction manifested in (for example) Heath-Stubbs's rearrangement of his Collected Poems and David Wright's complete disowning of his first collection.

There is a question as to whether this apologetic rearrangement of his oeuvre – like a deck of cards 'cut' down the middle – has done anything to help a reputation most of which (as he presciently joked in 'Epitaph') Heath-Stubbs outlived. Given how little change in style or theme there is to be found between the first and second sections of his Collected – a continuity apparently more evident to the reader than the author – I would suggest it has done little good, and may even have been detrimental by relegating some of his best poems to the obscurity of the middle pages.

In his preface to the Collected Poems, Heath-Stubbs is still to be found debating with his 'friend and contemporary at Oxford, Philip Larkin' (1988: 23), whom by then he had also outlived, as to the legitimacy of high-culture allusions in poetry. But whether his early style was too literary or not literary enough, Heath-Stubbs seems to have felt the sting of his younger rival's criticism. To adapt Churchill's words after El Alamein, Larkin's review may not have marked the end for Heath-Stubbs, or even the beginning of the end; but it was perhaps the end of the beginning.

WORKS CITED

Eliot, T. S. The Sacred Wood (London: Methuen, 1960).
Heath-Stubbs, John. A Charm Against the Toothache (London: Methuen, 1954).
—Collected Poems 1943–1987 (Manchester: Carcanet, 1988).
Larkin, Philip and Thwaite, Anthony (ed.). Collected Poems (London: Faber & Faber / Victoria: The Marvell Press, 2003).
—Further Requirements: Interviews, Broadcasts, Statements and Reviews, 1952–85 (London: Faber & Faber, 2002).
Lucie-Smith, Edward. British Poetry since 1945 (Harmondsworth: Penguin, 1970).
Motion, Andrew. Philip Larkin: A Writer's Life (London: Faber & Faber, 1993).
Szirtes, George. 'John Heath Stubbs', georgeszirtes.blogspot.co.uk/2008/10/john-heath-stubbs.html, 2008.
Wright, David. The Mid-Century: English Poetry 1940–60 (Harmondsworth: Penguin, 1965).

Three Poems

RORY WATERMAN

Kruja

'Skanderbeg's town' – and
there he is, terrible on his
plinth-top horse by the bankomat,
flanked by bee-lining stray dogs.

Where is the nearest button-shaped
Hoxha bunker? Look in be quick.
It is waist-deep in a wash
of soil and cigarette butts; and

all is as promised:

each knackered Mercedes
or Audi bucks at the corner,
throws its tails of dust
to the empty sky where

the castle tower sticks
from its clifftop, like a flexed digit.
Did we come to be different –
in and apart – and find it?

Spurn

Walk near that shifting tail and maybe you'll find
the ten-foot concrete disc from the Great War
lodged in a field, behind wire and under lichens:
a deaf ear to Deutschland. And, somewhere near,
a broad barn with its cracked corrugated roof,
by piles of worn-out tyres and mouldering dung.

We stop and startle twenty blinking Friesians
who step up to the gate for us, some huffing,
some grinding belch. Who know what they can count on:
the farmer coming each night, all clicks and whistles;
those steel bars and the sun, the sideways rain
beyond, with the field they once lay down in;

the jostling flanks of others; them being here –
and what? One licks her nose,
a slow pink swipe across a pad of black,
then clops away; then each in turn turns off,
like lights at night: when there's nothing to fear
why unite, why stay alert? One steps askance

and arcs her tail; a pile of slop claps down,
five taps, like irregular pentameter;
and others break off, get back to minding themselves.
Those once-high fields beyond their breezeblock walls
are pared back down to shoots, with little lakes
of standing water rimpling in the squalls,

full of jostling gulls. Beyond, a car brakes
to take the final bend, the mile to Kilnsea:
the last eked-out village, held both sides
by walls of concrete, then sand, to mark where sea
must turn. Where homesteads outstare each high tide.

Follow the waymarked trail out of the village

Mapless – but anyway we sought the iron-age fort
as gusts flung pompoms of mistletoe
in the apple trees up from the church; then
a kestrel was picking the thrust and stall of wind
above a lifeless field of waterlogged clods
(starlings had poured to a tuft in the mesh of hedge);
and next a copse, instant and dense,
hid a gap-toothed plough then behind it, dotting a clearing,
earth-caked pheasant feeders, by a downed once-electric fence
where KEEP OUT PRIVATE was nailed in high on a trunk;
tall beech saplings juddered, irate at each top,
and burnished leaves rotted in unflustered piles.
And here was the buck, gut loose as a bowl of cherries,
A tiny tumult rearranging in his eye.

Scanner

ADAM HEARDMAN

Drawing your attention to the number of frames
Per second, we turn the Muybridge-sequence each way,
Thinking of the difference between 'metres' and 'metres-per-second'.
Like no faces you've ever seen before, the faces
In Jacques-Louis David's unfinished *Oath in the Tennis Court* (1790–4)
Are torn on to their nudes, riffing on aspects of conjugation,
Of confluence. 'Look at how the never-living differ
From the dead', you said, 'and this other fine mess
You were about to have gotten me into'. Bit by bit
We unmade sense, and all the other kinds of trouble
You were about to have gotten me into. 'Bit by bit,

From the dead', you said, 'and this other fine mess
Of confluence.' Look at how the never-living differ,
Are torn onto their nudes, riffing on aspects of conjugation,
In Jacques-Louis David's unfinished *Oath in the Tennis Court* (1790–4),
Like no faces you've ever seen. Before the faces,
Thinking of the difference between 'metres' and 'metres-per-second-
Per-second', we turn the Muybridge-sequence each way,
      Drawing your attention to the number of frames.

~

Suppose the way you meant 'which way did you mean' finally
Struck me as important. Turning your watch's face away so I couldn't see
Reminded me to check the time, as if seeing
Into a room lit entirely from below a glass floor
By the light of a thousand bulbs. Like a pilot
Reading a sign saying 'Do Not Talk To The Pilot',
Or like waking up to that bit in *Memento* (2000), I woke
Up in a foot-chase, not knowing if I was chasing that guy
Or vice-versa. Nothing was resolved by the way we turned.
Which way did you mean you were reading a poem 'by yourself'?
Or vice-versa? Nothing was resolved by the way we turned
Up in a foot-chase, not knowing if I was chasing that guy
Or waking up to that bit in *Memento* (2000). I woke –
Reading a sign saying 'Do Not Talk To The Pilot'
By the light of a thousand bulbs, like a pilot –
Into a room lit entirely from below. A glass floor
Reminded me to check the time, as if 'seeing'
Struck me as important – turning your watch's face away so I couldn't see,
      Suppose, the way you meant. Which way did you mean 'finally'?

~

In the event of a crash I
Leave my honesty to the judge, my piety to the priest,
The sky to the pilot, my constant fear of falling to
The ground. You told me the empty wooden picture frame was a picture of
A picture, or at least a picture of a wooden frame, or, at least,
A tree. You told me the whole project was a mess.
Failure to have eyes in the back of my head led me into
The future. Failing to see through the glass I looked up
Into this sky, or down onto that universe. I missed
The future, failing to see through the glass. I looked up –
Failure to have eyes in the back of my head led me into
A tree. You told me the whole project was a mess,
A picture, or at least a picture of a wooden frame, or, at least,
The ground. You told me the empty wooden picture frame was a picture of
The sky, 'to the pilot'. My constant fear of falling/to
Leave; my honesty to the judge, my piety to the priest.
      In the event of a crash I

Syllabics

Psycho-Syllabics / Confessing to Syllabics

CLAIRE CROWTHER

'I, too, dislike it', wrote Marianne Moore, referring to poetry – and she must have included syllabic poetry because she was and remains its pre-eminent practitioner. Her opinion is not unusual. My impression is that contemporary syllabics, where the organisational principle in the line is the number of syllables, never was and still isn't popular. I hear conversations between poets about which journal editors won't accept a submission in syllabics. I know poets who write in syllabics but hate to be asked about it and dismiss the fact. Peter Groves has listed the judgments of anti-syllabicists including Basil Bunting ('silly'), Michael Hamburger ('cannot see the point'), Adrian Henri ('redundant'), Peter Levi ('uninteresting'), and John Heath-Stubbs ('totally spurious'). Thom Gunn, discounting his own superb examples, said he used syllabics only to get away from traditional English metre and onto free verse. Donald Hall described that process:

Syllabics was a way of holding on to number while avoiding iambic. I rhymed on the off-stress, pretending that English was French. From syllabics I took the leap to various types of free verse. I felt this necessity to break out of the cage I had made for myself [...]

Even this exercise-led approach to syllabics hasn't helped it. A creative writing MA student told me recently that her tutor had warned her against syllabics. She isn't sure why.

I also wonder. But then I'm fascinated by the syllable and all its actions. The syllable is the conventional, language-led atom in every English-language poem. Like any atom, it isn't the smallest bit of material, being typically a consonant plus a vowel plus perhaps another consonant. But it's wonderfully stretchy. It can be as simple as *O* and as convoluted as *Christ*. For this reason alone, counting a syllable as one unit can't confine a line any more than identifying a foot will straitjacket its rhythmic variety.

My fascination isn't new. Shaping a poetic line by counting the number of its syllables has been practised in too many languages to pick any out, though I'm learning Welsh because that's a language very close to the English border and its historic syllabic practice is clearly worth reading in the original. I don't include these practices in my narrow definition above of contemporary English-language syllabics. Languages have different ways of using syllables: weight, duration, stress, accent. There are hundreds of years of academic discussion about the English syllable which I occasionally dip into, for sport. Robert Bridges, poet laureate from 1915 to 1930, took syllables seriously. That was a period when poets and critics battled about the syllable's contribution to metre. Bridges tried using classical syllable effects in his major and most popular work, *The Testament of Beauty*. It's numbingly hard to read nowadays despite the appealing loss of final 'e's for short syllabled words like 'hav'. But Bridges's effort had one welcome result. It influenced his daughter, Elizabeth Daryush, who understood from her father that the normal speech stresses of English syllables could offer an exciting sound, and one differing from traditional metric verse. She also realised that a breakdown in regulation could push her poems into a post-First-World-War society.

Daryush is possibly the first English poet to write in modern syllabics. She attached a note to *Verses: Fourth Book* (1934), a collection mixing metrical poems with syllabic poems:

The poems without line-capitals are those written in syllabic metres (by which I mean metres governed only by the number of syllables to the line, and in which the number and position of the stresses may be varied at will) and are so printed as a reminder to the reader to follow strictly the natural speech-rhythm, and not to look for stresses where none are intended.

Her most famous and attractive use of syllabics, perhaps, is 'Still-Life':

Through the open French window the warm sun
lights up the polished breakfast table, laid
round a bowl of crimson roses, for one –
a service of Worcester porcelain, arrayed
near it a melon, peaches, figs, small hot
rolls in a napkin, fairy rack of toast,
butter in ice, high silver coffee-pot,
and, heaped on a salver, the morning's post.

(*Selected Poems,* Carcanet, 1972)

Conversational speech rhythm fights against the memory of metre in these lines. Matthew Francis, one of the most able of contemporary British syllabicists, echoes Daryush's reasoning: 'Avoiding metre is part of the point, because it allows a far greater rhythmic variety than is possible in metrical verse; I found my [syllabic] lines sounded more natural and conversational.' That's true in Daryush's stanza, and the sentence that composes the whole of it gains importance – but so do the less conversational end-rhymes and subtly patterned alliterations and assonances.

There is also a political point here, which Octavio Paz raised in an analysis of poetry and history: 'The importance of syllabic versification reveals the imperialism of discourse and grammar.' Latin languages, he said, are 'the offspring of Rome'. Paz meant non-English, weighted-language syllabicism.

But for those poets writing in a post-colonial setting, such as Zulfikhar Ghose, who supported modern English syllabics during a spat in the *Times Literary Supplement* in the 1960s, such formal reductionism controls the language of empire while it throws off imperialism. If Paz saw accentual poetry as rebelling against syllabically-controlled metres, Daryush and Ghose wanted to rebel against them too but used syllable count to do so. To clarify, Daryush adds a warning in her note: 'The bulk of English "syllabic" verse is, of course, not really syllabic in the strict sense, but more truly accentual.'

Pre-twentieth-century theorists had differentiated the two. W. H. Auden, who was influenced by Marianne Moore's syllabics, wrote a clerihew, presumably for students:

Among the prosodists, Bysshe
Was the syllable-counting old sissy
Guest
The accentual pest.

In 1583, far earlier than Edward Bysshe (1702, *The Art of Poetry*) and Victorian Edwin Guest, Sir Philip Sidney said: 'Now, of versifying, there are two sorts, the one ancient, the other modern; the ancient marked the quantity of each syllable and according to that, framed his verse, the modern observing only number (with some regard of the accent) [...]' and, again, he didn't mean by the latter what Daryush meant by syllabic poetry. He meant that accentual-syllabic poems count both syllables and beats. Later, accentual poems counted only beats. Free verse counts neither. Modern syllabic poems count only syllables.

To train the ear not to care that, outside a poem, you might not actually pronounce a phrase in such a way as fits a metrical pattern – to hear in your mind that phrase pronounced both ways at the same time, and without irritation – is just one of the wonders accentual-syllabic poets can perform. Free verse poets and syllabic poets must rely on unregularised speech stresses because they don't set up a metrical pattern that can drown out everyday speech.

But syllabics offers some glories. For one thing, it can work closely with the page. Cheap paper and the digital document have encouraged an exploitation of the space around words. In her zeal to represent the actuality of contemporary speech, Daryush, in her first quote above, shows she was driven past syllabics to typography. Her father also; *The Testament of Beauty* does not use line-capitals, his accentual lyrics do. This unnatural stress, which tips the balance of a line, remained popular for half a century more. Other poets, such as Dylan Thomas and Marianne Moore, used syllabics to dominate the page visually far more than Daryush. B.S. Johnson wrote, in his 'Note on Metre' in 1964:

Since most poetry reaches its audience in printed form, a metre which is easily apprehended visually, as any syllabic one is, would seem to be more appropriate than those metres which depend upon sound, like stress or quantitative ones.

In 'Ocean', for example, Matthew Francis creates a space suggesting both depth and surface well suited to a repeating multi-stanza of declining syllable-length lines:

The surface of the ocean. It's too deep here for waves.
There is only the slight swell that turns into them
thousands of miles away. A bubble rises,
which you'd never notice, except this time

you're closer to it than you might be
and have been to where it came from.
Now it's dispersed in the air –

another ocean, or
part of the same one,

the deep blue world.

The cinquain, a much-loved syllabic form invented by Adelaide Crapsey, who died in 1914, seems to rustle the paper it's written on:

NIGHT WINDS

The old
Old winds that blew
When chaos was, what do
They tell me the clattered trees that I
Should weep?

This syllabic pattern is 2 4 6 8 2 and it is scenically intense. Interestingly, 'Night Winds' allows two meanings to emerge from the final line, governed by reading a stress on the first or second word. Is the poet being told to weep? Or told something that makes her weep? There is an iambic lilt throughout and its echo suggests the latter but the syllabic pattern, picking out the contested phrase in two confronted syllables, helps resist this. That is a strength here, in my view, and Crapsey must have intended the double effect in a poem that is wholly governed by a question asked in a reflective syntax.

A long cinquain-repeating poem, such as Rachel Wetzsteon's 'Commands for the End of Summer', gives the reader an internal sense of the 2 4 6 8 2 rhythm as much as a metre could. And here is a problem: what if Wetzsteon had varied one of the stanzas to be, instead, 2 4 4 8 2? Many would denounce this. Should not simple things – and counting has a nursery plainness about it – be pure? But if lines that are iambic pentameters may be purely iambic for, say, as little as twenty-five percent of the time, because monotony is fatal and the mind establishes a pattern at the beginning of the poem and deals with variety very well thereafter, then why is it a problem that the syllabic line occasionally varies from its set pattern? Is this because the reader can't hear most syllabic lines in the way you hear an iambic line and therefore the reader has to trust the poet to deliver the number of syllables promised – and when you find the number is out by three you feel duped? Though why should you, if the poem is successful as a whole? Many excellent syllabics-controlled poems offer occasional miscounted lines. Matthew Francis points out, 'both Daryush and W. D. Snodgrass miscount the syllables in places, and the fact that this doesn't make any real difference to the effect of the poem is an interesting theoretical problem'. Miscounting, anyway, is an opportunity to make a point to the reader, even if the point is not understood for a while afterwards.

But this is not, perhaps, the major source of argument between syllabics-lovers and naysayers. The question that has not, possibly cannot be answered satisfactorily, is this: how do you define or categorise contemporary syllabics? Is it, helpfully, a metre? Some say yes because metre means counting and a syllabic poet counts syllables, of course. B.S. Johnson defended what the *Spectator* had referred to in 1962 as a 'new fad':

Defining metre as the meaningful arrangement in regular patterns of one (or, rarely, more) of the constituent elements of language, it is as legitimate to use syllables as the elements from which to form metrical units as it is to use elements like stress or quantity.

But many believe such a form is not truly measured because you do not hear the count of syllables. In that case, the syllabic poem is actually free verse. At perhaps a bathetic level, which such arguments tend to reach, at least there is more measure in a syllabic line or set of lines than in prose. In fact, if you use a regular five-syllable line, you will hear a two-beat metre in the background, as many on both sides of the argument have pointed out. The ten-syllable line offers the choice of an occasional strict pentameter and it's easy to pattern in lines with odd numbers of syllables when you want to switch off the musicality. Though, if you read enough, let's say, thirteen-syllable lines, you will start to recognise them.

But the rhythm of syllabics is, in a way, discounted and, says critic Timothy Steele, there being no pattern of accent is a principle of syllabic verse. Steele's point is an important one. Just when you begin to discern a regular iambic or trochaic line, you will be thrown off course. Key poets in the prehistory of modern syllabics understood this. John Donne added meaning to his critique of courtly life when he subverted the pentameter so completely that he was accused of only counting syllables, in lines worse than deficient metrically:

Then man is a world; in which, Officers
Are the vast ravishing seas; and Suiters,
Springs; now full, now shallow, now drye; which, to
That which drowns them, run. These self reasons do
Prove the world a man, in which, officers
Are the devouring stomacke, and Suiters
The excrements, which they voyd. All men are dust
('Satyre V')

Marianne Moore also knew that what you hear, together with what you see on the page, can make a pleasing and accurate dissonance. You look at her famously complex one-off stanza patterns of syllabically-counted lines while hearing natural-sounding long sentences. Here are the last three stanzas of 'The Fish':

All
external
    marks of abuse are present on this
    defiant edifice –
        all the physical features of

ac-
cident – lack
    of cornice, dynamite grooves, burns, and
    hatchet strokes, these things stand
        out on it; the chasm-side is

dead.
Repeated
    evidence has proved that it can live
    on what can not revive
        its youth. The sea grows old in it.

Moore used syllabics to whip up lines from material found in scientific prose. So does David Morley, as he explains here:

Take any good field guide you have to hand and open it at random. You will find precise, and sometimes magically incisive, description, and names that seem to fall from fairytales, and a language as precise as it is strange to the ear. In the following example, I have broken some prose verbatim into counted syllabic lines; I have placed episodes of linked description into stanzas, and lineated in a way which forces the eye to move around the page to find connections and answers. Nevertheless, it could also stand as prose given the right context; little has been changed:

EUROPEAN LARCH

The Alps –
replaced by Norway Spruce
in colder, wetter areas –
with ranges
in the Tatra and Sudetan
plains and mountains of Poland.
Long cultivated and abundant:
in older plantations, shelterbeds
and parks,
away from cities and the driest, drabbest areas.

Timber
tough and rot-resistant;
Tatra and Sudetan forms make
the finest
variety plantation trees.
Variants: 'Pendula', that
broad and depressed-looking tree displays
exaggeratedly weeping shoots;
most rare;
even rarer, spectacularly weeping cultivars

Coming at that choice of syllabics for prose from another position, W. D. Snodgrass said: 'I chose [the purely syllabic metric] for my poem, hoping it might open some new rhythmic possibilities to me, but hoping also that it would let me drop into occasional stretches of flat prose which might balance the rather "poetical" quality of the images I had collected.'

This dulling of the poetical has intrigued poets as different as W. H. Auden and Philip Levine, and has been found useful in a variety of styles, from traditional lyrics such as Simon Armitage's 'Goalkeeper with a Cigarette', to radical conceptual offerings such as Kenneth Goldsmith's *No. 111.2.7.93 – 10.20.96/6,* which arranges read and transcribed texts by number of syllables. In this poem, entries of one syllable compose chapter one, two-syllable entries compose chapter two, etc. Raymond McDaniel, reviewing Goldsmith's work, refers to this syllabic tour de force as 'obsessive'. It may be that the fact that syllabic patterns are number-based, a use of number with no other rhythmic requirement, strikes readers as obsessive. But this is an argument that could be used about the usually well-regarded approaches of Oulipo, a group that believes constraint aids creativity.

Besides, number can be poetic. A poet might want to employ the rich symbolism of number for a poem as Sylvia Plath did in 'Metaphors', a nine-line poem about pregnancy, with nine syllables per line. And it's not just to accommodate number that poets drop syllables from the beginning of words (apheresis) or the end (apocope) in ways once thought beautiful but that can now sound unacceptably poetic. In a poem narrated by a pig going to the abattoir, the use Philip Levine makes of central-syllable reduction (syncope), to suggest a socio-political reality, is delicately poetic:

> In my dreams
> the snouts drool on the marble
> suffering children, suffering flies,
>
> suffering the consumers
> who won't meet their steady eyes
> for fear they could see.
> ('Animals Are Passing from Our Lives')

The word 'suffering' can be pronounced with either two or three syllables. Given the seven-syllable repeating line, the first two uses of 'suffering' must be read with two syllables and the third with three syllables. The word is thus drawn out to enhance the irony on which the poem is founded: consumers/bosses, whose choice it is to eat pork and ignore animal/worker suffering, cause greater suffering than flies or children. They know dead pigs/workers suffer. The pigs suffer twice but the word 'suffering' for them loses a syllable, twice, and is dematerialised. It is the three-syllabled suffering of the consumers which must be borne in the market of meat-eaters to which pigs and workers must go: 'I'm to market', says the narrator. Thus this poem, about capital and the relations of labour to the market, evolves its metaphor through its syllabics.

Levine's poem depicts the brio of suffering and the form supports that, as it does poems that engage with suffering only on a cognitive level. While they do not offer a guide to meaning, as heavy metrical feet do, nor autonomy to the line as free verse does, syllabically counted lines allow the qualities of hesitancy and unstated order to fit poems to our era of philosophic stress. Is truth a meaningless cultural structure, like syllabics?

There are mathematical applications of syllabics, such as Tony Leuzzi's series of poems based on Pi, but a syllabic poem is not always a wholly confident presentation of counting in the way maths is. I find that the relation of the syllabic count to lines is more like the clutch of a hand on a swaying rope bridge over a deep chasm – not sure of itself at all.

But I'm reversing roles here. The line is vulnerable while the count is remorseless. Roselle Brown says of her book *Cora Fey*: 'I chose syllabics as a form partly because that meant I would have to ration my words. They would be very dear, they would be very costly. Every time I wanted an adjective I would have to beg for it in my syllabic line.'

Goldsmith's shattering of our cultural icons by number, Moore's cold and cutting enjambment, a line torn at 'on' or 'a', a word ripped into parts, shredded syntax bleeding down a page: these syllabic executions turn the reader's eye toward the line ending, not away from it, and toward the night. Syllabic poems make good chillers. What is a syllabic line but an impure hybrid of irregular rhythm and ghosting metre? What does a stanza in contemporary syllabics sound like but an interstitial strophe? Monstrosities, both. Michael Waters uses his characteristic ten-syllable line to freezing effect:

> The Baptist's beheaded Arab fashion:
> Throat slit with the long sword, then the gristly
> Tendons of the neck severed with the knife
> Still sheathed behind this executioner's
> Back – the beheading's not quite over yet,
> Like the tape loop broadcast on CNN
> ('Michelangelo Merisi Da Caravaggio', *Gospel Night*)

Waters' syllabic devices are not overdone; they stabilise horror with the dulled unemotional handcuffing of each line. The line could go on and say more but it's not allowed. And there's no point. Given it takes three seconds to pronounce a syllable (whatever its length by letter) and thirty seconds is the limit of our attention span, a ten-syllable line constitutes the limit of the auditory moment, as Frederick Turner and Ernst Pöppel have suggested. Just when a listener can't take any more of Waters' material, the horrified brain stops listening. But the horrifying number starts again, conscripting the reader. Syllabics is a good choice for this interplay between meaningless neural experience and the build of an uncomfortable poem. Anyway, after the first line beats a regular, breezy and short swipe of the cultural knife, and the second identical number of syllables delivers a long killing thrust ending on the almost forcefully separated syllables of 'gristly', the remaining lines sound too tired to be pacey. Expectation, which is delivered by metrical beat and is similar to hope, is stripped away. The last line drags its feet. It has nothing rhythmic to offer.

While here and there in quiet corners poets are keeping calm by counting, I don't see syllabics as a peaceful practice. It is more likely the psychopathy of the line and possibly this is why so many poets dislike it.

REVIEWS

Mixed Up Confucian

A. D. Moody, *Ezra Pound: Poet – A Portrait of the Man & his Work. Volume III: The Tragic Years*

Oxford University Press 2015
654 + xxii pp., £30

Reviewed by MATTHEW CREASY

As news of the Japanese attack on Pearl Harbour reached Italy in early 1942, Reynolds Packard, the director of the United Press in Rome, tried to warn Ezra Pound about the consequences of his continuing public support for Mussolini's government. The American poet was, however, obdurate: 'But I believe in Fascism [...]. And I want to defend it.' Pound saw the broadcasts he made on Rome Radio as a matter of free speech: he wished to show Americans that their involvement in the war was misguided; that they had been led astray by the monopolising activities and usurious practices of various wealthy Jewish interests.

Pound thought of himself as a free agent, but the Italian Ministry for Popular Culture described him as 'a collaborator' in December 1943. The phrase was, A. David Moody explains, ambiguous: 'In Italian, as in English, *collaboratore* can mean "a colleague, a co-worker", as well as "one who works with the enemy".' The word admits, Moody suggests, 'a sense of Pound's compromised situation'. Such attention to nuance characterises Moody's general approach to writing Pound's life, an enterprise completed with the publication of *The Tragic Years,* covering 1939 to 1972.

Even 'fascism' receives scrutiny. By August 1936, Dorothy Pound was already complaining to her husband that the word was becoming 'hopelessly vulgarised' within press coverage of the Spanish Civil War. As Moody explains, the couple were concerned about the way that 'fascism' ceased to connote identifiable political values and was being used as a purely pejorative epithet. (It is broadly in this sense that Hilary Benn described Daesh as 'fascists' to the House of Commons on 2 December 2015.) The risk, Pound felt, was that 'significant distinctions were being lost in the clash and confusion of ideologies'.

Pound's polemics against usury were not, however, free from their own confusions and conflations, witnessed by his repeated recourse to stereotype in both poetry and prose. Reading through his life becomes an exhausting catalogue of obstinate and blinkered unpleasantness. Having previously written with care and sensitivity about Pound's anti-Semitism, Moody's final volume begins by covering the broadcasts made in support of Mussolini on Rome Radio from 1941 to 1943, before detailing Pound's arrest and internment at a prison camp outside Pisa and arrangements for his trial upon charges of treason in America after the war. Defining the nature of Pound's involvement with fascism is such an important part of these events that Moody's index to this volume includes a subentry for 'Fascism [...] distinguished from "fascism"' within his treatment of Pound's politics.

Amongst other reasons, a fuller understanding of Pound's political views is important to understanding his guilt relative to the charges of treason brought against him. The F.B.I. started accumulating files on him before America had even entered the war; one of Pound's earliest and most assiduous bibliographers was Frank Amprim, the agent assigned to his case, who kept copious records of his published and unpublished writings. Despite the evidence accumulated by Amprim, Moody argues that the case against Pound was not a strong one. First, there was a paucity of witnesses: radio engineers flown over from Italy spoke little English and could provide only disconnected testimony about his broadcasting activities; next, the laws against treason held that acts against the state should be 'intentional': Pound maintained that he never sought 'to strengthen the enemy or weaken the power to resist him' as the law required; finally, Moody questions whether Pound *was* a fascist, arguing that his investment in doctrines of individual responsibility owed more to Confucius. If Pound had ever made it to trial, it is likely that the prosecution would have been unsuccessful and Moody cites an unpublished state memo from 1950 to this effect.

In this account, Pound's politics are 'too complicated for any simple judgement'. Although sympathetic, Moody is clear-eyed about where Pound went wrong, was mistaken or merely plain vicious. But importantly, his attention to nuance extends to readings of Pound's poetry too. Moody's account of Canto 74 as 'a complex and extended musical composition' is characteristic of his approach throughout all three volumes. Even from Pound's earliest work, Moody reads the structure of his poetry attentively, tracing the implications of pattern and juxtaposition. His skill as a critic is to unpick the logic that underpins the collocation of Pound's seemingly disparate material within the *Cantos*. Usefully, he's also clear about where this tips into obscurity, especially in some of the later Cantos. Pound wrote, Moody indicates, for the army of explicators who would follow.

If Pound inspired the New Critics, his work also divided opinion. Three years before he was awarded the Bollingen Prize for *Pisan Cantos*, a group of Marxist writers vigorously debated whether Pound deserved the death penalty in *New Masses*: 'Because he was a poet his crime was millionfold. Because he is a traitor he should be shot.' During the 1950s, however, pressure increased to secure his release. Official testimony that he was insane came from Dr Winfred Overholser, at the instigation of Pound's defence attorney, Julian Cornell, who had been engaged by his publisher and former protégé, James Laughlin, of New Directions. If anyone emerges from this account as a villain it is Overholser, who went to considerable lengths to secure the declaration of insanity, against the findings of his own colleagues. Although this meant Pound was spared the possibility of the death penalty, it also deprived him, as Moody sees it, of the chance to vindicate himself in court. And it created problems in securing his release: if he were truly insane, then he should stay locked up, if not, should he face the trial he had avoided? As it was, he was confined at St Elizabeths hospital, outside Washington, longer than any prison sentence associated with the charges against him.

The matter of Pound's sanity is nearly as complex and delicate as the question of his politics. He certainly suffered breakdowns under the pressure of events; but the diagnosis largely came down to the fact that he was obsessive about his economic theories and failed to grasp the point of view of others. There are signs, too, that he colluded in the continuing diagnosis of insanity. For life in St Elizabeths was relatively comfortable: Pound

was able to write; he held court over groups of hangers-on who came to visit him; and he struck up relationships with women such as Sheri Martinelli and Marcella Spann who inspired him to creativity. Nevertheless, the repercussions of his official mental status were longstanding. He wasn't released from the 'bughouse' until 1958 and handing over legal responsibility for his affairs to his wife later allowed her to disregard instructions in his will regarding the disposal of his literary estate after his death in 1972.

On leaving St Elizabeths, Pound moved back to Italy, taking his wife and Marcella. Breaking up this strange ménage, Marcella's departure seems to have induced a final crisis. Pound retreated to his daughter Mary's family home in Germany, and then returned to his longstanding mistress Olga Rudge's apartment in Venice where he began writing apologetic letters to old friends, like Richard Aldington and T. S. Eliot. He met with Alan Ginsberg in 1967, to whom he declared: 'my worst mistake was the stupid suburban prejudice of anti-Semitism'. Ginsberg's reply – 'Ah, that's lovely to hear you say that [...] as it says in I Ching, "No Harm"' – may provoke mixed feelings. For once, Moody doesn't comment. His monumental biography is so judicious and scrupulous that it allows readers to decide for themselves if this late repentance constitutes sufficient atonement.

Squandering No Light

Kathleen Jamie
The Bonniest Companie
Picador, £9.99

Reviewed by SUE LEIGH

In 2014, a year of tremendous energy in Scotland, Kathleen Jamie decided to participate in her own way, as a lyric poet: 'I wanted to embrace that energy [...] I resolved to write a poem a week, following the cycle of the year'. She called the forty-seven poems written over the course of 2014, *The Bonniest Companie* (the words are borrowed from the Scottish Border ballad 'Tam Lin' where the Queen of the Fairies rages against the aristocratic young Janet: 'She has ta'en awa the bonniest knight / in a' my companie').

The discipline of writing in such a structured way might have produced a collection that is uniform, but it is richly various. Jamie is known for her lyrical, reflective poems and prize-winning collections of essays *Findings* and *Sightlines,* which offer a visionary response to the natural world while drawing attention to our fragile relationship with it. There are a number of poems of this kind in the book, many about birds. 'Migratory I', for example, describes a dead whooper swan, its wing 'wind-fit, quartz-bright [...] A radiant gate / one could open and slip through'.

In the first of two 'Eyrie' poems she writes, 'I was feart we'd lost the falcons' but 'here she is! Conjured out of drizzle / and March mist, her yellow claws / a holdfast on the rock's edge.'

There are, unsurprisingly, strong political undercurrents to the collection. In 'The Hinds' – a poem that recreates the creatures' agility in its fluid shape – the deer are 'at their ease, alive / to lands held on long lease'. And in '23/9/14' (the Scottish independence referendum was held on 18/9/14) the poem's mood shifts from 'tattered hopes' to the determined conclusion, 'Today we begin again.' She makes us aware, however, that the political – 'us and all our works' – is always provisional. The wider horizon has to be kept open; the natural world is bigger than politics.

The challenge of writing a poem a week encouraged Jamie to venture into new territory. The poems in this collection not only look towards the future but back into the past – to her largely urban childhood. 'I haven't thought of you in years', she says of 'the world tree' that grew at the bottom of their lane, 'but wonder now what kind you were / – elder or hawthorn, bour or may / – and why I suddenly care.' Two Corporation Road poems imagine a child in a vast universe – in the first she is carried in her father's arms to see 'the stars above the steelworks' glare'; in the second, she 'birded up' into the sky on her red swing, 'come back, said the Earth, / I have your shadow'. In 'Homespun' she wonders what happened to her mother's hand-knits, the lamp decorated with shells she had collected, 'squandering no light'.

The poem-a-week discipline, Jamie says, had an impact on her writing method. She did not redraft in the same way – preferring instead to follow the idea, 'the first mark, the right mark'. In doing so she sacrificed the well-wrought poem for a freer, looser style, making it easier to access her own cadences, her own speaking – and poetic – voice. She slips in and out of her native Scots ('Thon blackbird'), and the handful of poems entirely in Scots are deliberately not glossed. There is freshness, a supple energy, in these poems with their short and long lines, exclamation marks and questions – we are listening to the poet 'caught mid-thought, mid-dash', as she says of the shrew found dead on the path.

Although not overtly stated, the poems are located in time, following the seasons. 'Glacial', a winter poem, looks out from the top of a hill in Fife and considers the Romans who 'came, saw, / and soon thought the better of' and forward to when the lynx, and possibly the wolf, might be re-introduced in Scotland. In two early summer poems, 'Arbour' and 'Garden', the poet attends minutely to the world but questions what she knows of it. And in 'Blossom' she chastises herself for not paying more attention, 'How many May dawns / have I slept right through, / the trees courageous with blossom?'

The Bonniest Companie is a remarkable response to the events of a remarkable year. We could do worse than respond to Jamie's suggestion in 'The Cliff' to 'take our chances here with the mortal, / the common and the mortal, [...] / and let space open / between word and world / wind-strummed, trembling'.

Vision & Vacuity

Harold Bloom, *The Daemon Knows: Literary Greatness and the American Sublime*
Oxford University Press
£22.50

Reviewed by
NICOLAS TREDELL

'Without vision, criticism perishes.' This aphorism in Harold Bloom's latest book is the credo that underpins his life's work. But it is a reversible claim: without criticism, vision may perish, dissolving into the intense inane. Like Bloom's other books from *The Western Canon* (1994) onwards, *The Daemon Knows* aspires to the condition of vision but sometimes balloons into the empyrean where sight strains to perceive shape, or falls, deflated, to earth. We expect late Bloom to be overblown; but a more focused book might have conveyed his key ideas and insights – he still has some – more forcefully.

The core of Bloom's argument is that twelve writers created the American sublime and represent 'our incessant effort to transcend the human without forsaking humanism'. As he puts it, in what he admits is a simplistic way: 'the sublime in literature has been associated with peak experiences that render a secular version of a theophany', a visible manifestation of God or a god to humankind: 'a sense of something interfused that transforms a natural moment, landscape, action or countenance'. As the allusion to 'Tintern Abbey' indicates, the sublime is not confined to the USA: but, for Bloom, 'America, the Evening Land, favours more drastic sublimities than Europe, abrupt splendours such as Dickinson's "certain slant of light" or Stevens's auroras', both of which are 'illuminations of discontinuity'.

Bloom divides his designated dozen into pairs and devotes a chapter to each duo: Whitman and Melville, Emerson and Dickinson (the one woman), Hawthorne and Henry James, Twain and Frost, Stevens and T. S. Eliot, Faulkner and Bloom's favourite, Hart Crane. He identifies the 'common element in these twelve writers' – though it is covert in Eliot – as 'their receptivity to daemonic influx'. Bloom's implied cognitive claim for the daemonic is summed up in his book's title: the daemon knows. Daemonic influx offers a gnosis, a form of knowledge, which is otherwise inaccessible.

The quality of Bloom's treatment of his twelve writers is, perhaps inevitably, uneven. He is better on poetry than prose, inclining, despite copious quotations, more to generalities with the latter; he shows greater insight into Crane and Stevens than into Whitman and Dickinson. Perhaps the strangest element in the book is his attitude to Eliot, which is, as he acknowledges, '[e]ndlessly ambivalent'. He sets up an agon between Eliot and Stevens in which Stevens emerges as more fecund, but he grudgingly admits the former to the pantheon of great American poets, 'very much in the High Romantic tradition of Shelley and Whitman'. His peroration on Eliot, however, denounces his 'dogmatism, dislike of women, debasement of ordinary human existence' and 'virulent anti-Semitism' and ends with the assertion that '[w]e do not read only as aesthetes – though we should – but also as responsible men and women. By that standard, Eliot, despite his daemonic gift, is unacceptable once and for all time'. The problem here – implicitly acknowledged in the interpolation 'though we should' – is that this is the very kind of denunciation that Bloom, in this and other recent books, has condemned as an importation of the ideological into the aesthetic.

There is another book in *The Daemon Knows* struggling to get out: a memoir of a life in reading and criticism which is adumbrated here in fragmentary, non-linear form but which it is tempting to reassemble as an outline for a portrait of the critic as a young man. For example, Bloom recalls how he discovered and started to read Hart Crane in the Melrose branch of the Bronx Public Library on his tenth birthday, 11 July 1940, and how his sisters pooled their cash to buy him a copy of Crane's *Collected Poems*, the first book he ever owned, for his twelfth birthday on 11 July 1942; he evokes himself as 'a poetry-haunted boy of thirteen walking about the Jewish East Bronx of 1943'; he recounts how he was introduced to Faulkner's work by the copy of Malcolm Cowley's *The Portable Faulkner* he bought when he turned sixteen on 11 July 1946; he remembers going up to Cornell where 'a great teacher, William M. Sale, Jr.', taught him 'how to read prose fiction'; he recollects, at the age of nineteen, meeting Wallace Stevens, who proved '[g]racious and benign'. Perhaps most memorably, he conjures up Young Bloom at New Haven:

A Yiddish-speaking Bronx proletarian, arriving at Yale as a twenty-one-year-old enthusiast of Blake, Shelley, Hart Crane, Stevens, Yeats, Hardy, Pater, Ruskin, Whitman, Spenser, and Milton, was not made welcome by an English faculty dominated by neo-Christian New Critics of the Eliotic persuasion: Cleanth Brooks and Robert Penn Warren, Maynard Mack and Louis Martz, William Wimsatt and René Wellek and their ephebes and camp followers. Rough, shaggy, parenthetical, self-conscious, and amiably polemical, I alienated most of them and would not have survived past a year but for the encouragement and kindness of two distinguished scholars, Dean William Clyde DeVane and Professor Frederick Albert Pottle.

Bloom also summons up encounters with a range of other critics and writers including M. H. Abrams, Kenneth Burke, Dorothea Krooke, Robert Frost, John Crowe Ransom, Robert Penn Warren, and his 'antithetical friend, the formidable Frank Kermode' with whom he shared an enthusiasm for Stevens but differed about the interpretation and evaluation of his poems. All these memories are framed by our narrator, who styles himself 'Old Bloom', a 'worn-out ancient exegete', who often reminds us of his age by reiterating the phrase 'at eighty-four', and who now, because of his physical frailty, conducts seminars in his 'large New England shingle house' rather than on university premises.

As these passages accumulate, the question presses: why doesn't Old Bloom write autobiography all-out? He offers an indirect answer to this when he quotes Oscar Wilde's remark that criticism is 'the only civilised form of autobiography' and states his own 'firm conviction that true criticism recognises itself as a mode of memoir'. But criticism perhaps works best in this way when direct autobiography is avoided; certainly the general effect of the autobiographical divagations in this book is one of rambling – or, at best, reminiscence work. *The Daemon Knows* is an amphibium – not great, though sometimes true – which wanders, restless and uneasy, between the diverse elements of autobiography and anthology, criticism and crypticity, and vision and vacuity.

Shaping a Republic

Jon Silkin, *Complete Poems*, edited by Jon Glover and Kathryn Jenner
Northern House/ Carcanet
2015

Reviewed by OWEN LOWERY

The title of Jon Silkin's *Complete Poems* is an understandable misnomer. In compiling this vast selection of work by a long-lived, productive and latterly neglected poet, Jon Glover and Kathryn Jenner had to choose among so many drafts and alternative versions that, as Glover says, 'it was difficult, and on occasion impossible, to decide which version to include'. The editors also worked through a hundred metres of archived material. The *Complete Poems* is far more comprehensive than previous volumes, such as the 1980 *Selected*.

This book adds to Silkin's published collections much previously unpublished material, presented in chronological groupings that appear immediately after corresponding books. It starts with Silkin's earliest collections, *The Portrait* (1950) and *The Peaceable Kingdom* (1954). A dialogue develops, across Silkin's half-century career, between his

seen and previously unseen work, and leaves the reader wondering why the poet did not collect so many effective poems. It also means that we must temper our views of less successful poems and regard them as part of a working process, but one that bears witness to the extraordinary productivity of a mind seemingly compelled to write. The appendices include alternative drafts of 'The Jews in England', 'A good farmer', and 'Air that Pricks Earth with Life'. Occasionally variations of a poem appear in parallel. In the case of 'Air that Pricks Earth with Life', Glover tell us, 'Silkin had been working on it for around five years' before it appeared in its entirety.

The result is a body of work that includes numerous notable highlights, is thematically eclectic, bears witness to a committed human and social code, and experiments with structured forms, free verse, and sequential poems. In 'Six Stanzas' Silkin uses six complete, numbered, but irregular stanzas to wrestle with the connected ideas of sex, nature, and creativity. Silkin shifts between arguments and ideas within more or less regular parameters, approaching and re-approaching his central themes from different angles, in the manner of a poetic philosopher, or a philosophical poet. The sequence becomes a quest for increasing clarity, and definition. Similar occurs in the six-part poem 'To Come Out Singing'. The form again follows the direction of Silkin's quest to make sense of life, whether or not that ambition succeeds.

Complete Poems affirms Silkin's place as an important Anglo-Jewish poet, whose themes include personal love and loss, social injustice, the relation between human and natural worlds, war, the Holocaust, and other languages and cultures. Glover's informative introduction underlines how Silkin, a friend, colleague, and former fellow-editor of *Stand*, was willing to submit poems to literary publications worldwide, from Britain and the United States to Japan, Australia, Sweden and elsewhere, exerting an important international influence. This book alerts us to the fact that Silkin's internationalism extends even to his final and most personal collection, *Making a Republic* (2002). In the free-verse poem 'Lament', private recollection and imagery combine with the private and public shadows of the Shoah, reflecting an identification with the Jewish victims of the Nazis. Released from rhythmic and metrical constraints, the opening image is sinister: 'In the kitchen a gas flame / blows away. Hissing toxicity', only partially mitigated by the speaker's domestic memories. The theme of irreconcilable loss crystallises: 'Where are you going, / mother, father, so soon / departing?', followed by the plea to his parents to

Stay,
there
is a little
thunderous dew,
so silent
this late summer
morning.

In 'Fire', longer lines are used to similar effect, as the loss is revisited. Here, though, there is the possibility of reconciliation, as Silkin dreams of his cremated father, bridging the chasm between life and death, and begging him to 'Come again in my lifetime, / where you need not speak, as often we did not.'

History and war also continue to have an impact in 'A Short Poem for Hiroshima'. Again prioritising syntax over formality, the poem marvels at the massive repercussions of activity, even on an atomic scale, reinforcing the sense that everything is connected, that any action has consequences:

Over the steps of a bank
flesh melts into shadow, no,
for that is absence of light – into concrete,
by a severed atom.

The same is true of the previously-unpublished poem 'Moon snow', in which the poet serves as the reader's guide to post-Bomb Japan, while empathising until he too becomes one of the victims:

In the city, charred fatty clothing
with merged globules of hair, the body's shade
fixed to a broken wall. I'm dust and light.

This mutuality has literary implications. As Silkin notes in 'Shaping a Republic', 'our poems will, in amiable / opposed passions, discuss each other',

whether they are those of 'the school room – Hokkaido', or those of 'a silent Newcastle night'.

In a further example of Silkin's free verse, 'The Fireflies of Minsk', the Holocaust is confronted from the outset in the form of 'Frail monoxides', and 'two men', who

watch these lives, who see
themselves watched,
as they gas.

The murderers watch the consequences of their deeds, and are seen for what they are by the eyes of poetry and history. What they do has universal consequence, as 'The soul is ghosted from its flesh', or, in 'Moon snow', the Holocaust is realised in the image of 'bodiless coats', and a symbolic re-opening of 'the rusted-up but still viable chambers of Maidanek', along with 'the roasters of Buchenwald'. The impact of historical events, therefore, ripples through Silkin's poetry, and is felt at a personal, emotional level, as well as being subject to philosophical exploration.

Despite the more obvious stanzaic regularity of much of Silkin's earlier poetry, it is not surprising that his concern with the human condition is also apparent there. In *The Portrait*, and *The Peaceable Kingdom*, the theme is explored through man's relations with the natural world. A poignant case in point is 'The Cunning of an Age'. Beginning with the narrative tone of parable or traditional Jewish story-telling, it presents an anthropomorphised fox that becomes an epitome of the seemingly ubiquitous hunted victim, the unending human capacity to inflict harm:

And the wind changed his name
To FOLLOWED from Fox-on-the-hill
And the wind followed, curling his brush. And the hounds followed too,
Like dreams like death on the hill.

The connection is firmly established in the stanzas of 'No Land Like it', where Silkin identifies directly with the figure of the harried fox:

But I a fox am bred
From out a hollow land of horns groined red
With hounds and men and secret faith and trysts
Beneath my orphanage of angry hills.

Silkin also identifies with working-class life and the world of manual labour, from the bargeman of 'Gurney's Poem', who 'smudges his fag in oil and clay', to his own grandfather as he 'backed a horse between his cart's shafts, / and tarpaulin keeping rain off wallpapers', in 'The line'. Silkin draws on his experiences of the 'slog' at 'Swan Hunter', 'where we build naval craft', and in the 'Killhope Wheel' poems, or as a grave-digger in 'Urban Grasses':

With a sickle, I tended the dead in London
shortening the grass that had flowered
on their bodies, as it had in my child's.
And I piled the soil over the paupers' flesh
in their flimsy coffins, which split.

Allied to this empathy is a profound moral concern, the perception of injustice in 'The Cunning of an Age', or 'The Malabestia', the title of which, Silkin notes, is derived from 'the name subsequently put onto Richard of Acaster', responsible for the murder of the three Jewish women previously spared during the slaughter of the Jews of York, in 1190. In Part 2 of 'Beneath the Hedgerows', Silkin's commitment is evident in his willingness to voice more recent social concerns:

There is paucity in the land;
Many are unemployed,
and we suffer at the hands of the police and the military.

Even as it provides an overview of the development of the themes of Silkin's poems, *Complete Poems* affords the opportunity to consider possible explanations for these themes. The recurring presence of the death of his one-year-old son, most famously lamented in 'Death of a son', but also apparent in 'For a mad child among mad children', and 'For David Emmanuel', is at the core of his concerns. Silkin's son died in a mental hospital, having been certified, and, like murdered Jews, exploited workers, and the poor in cheap, broken coffins, can be numbered among the victims of circumstance, bureaucracy and cruelty, as the poet reflects in Glover's Introduction:

Adam – that was the child's name – when he was nearly one year old, was summoned by County Hall, together with his mother, to come in order that he might be Certified. And what happened was that the mother and the child were kept waiting in a draughty corridor for about four hours and Adam caught pneumonia and died shortly afterwards.

Silkin's responses to this avertible loss are remarkable, and their pathos can encompass the whole of victimised, hunted humanity. Alongside his formal inventiveness, and his productivity, it is this universal compassion that is most obvious in *Complete Poems*, and throughout Silkin's *oeuvre*.

The Poetry and Poetics of Michael Heller
A Natural Memory
Edited by JON CURLEY and BURT KIMMELMAN

Moving On

The Poetry and Poetics of Michael Heller, edited by Jon Curley & Burt Kimmelman. Fairleigh Dickinson University Press, 2015, 204 pp.

Reviewed by IAN BRINTON

In the Preface to his collection of essays on 'Poets, Poetry and Poetics', published by Salt in 2005, Michael Heller suggested that 'Poetry is always about to happen and also about to disappear, to be drowned out by conventional thought, to marginalise itself or to be marginalised by its writers, readers and critics.' The poet who translates silence into audibility, the nameless into the named, the invisible into that which can be seen and read, recognises the way in which great compositions induce a sense of loneliness when they are contemplated. In Heller's own words from an interview with the editors of this fine new collection of essays, the loneliness is located in the moment of finishing the composition 'because when finished, they are separated' from those who created them:

The feel of closure, of the little box clicking shut, as Eliot speaks of it, has been one of the reasons for pursuing poetry. This has nothing to do with whether or not one is working in so-called closed or open forms; rather, closure is deeply a part of human experience, enabling us to understand, to 'move on' as the pop-lingo has it.

In the Foreword to the eight substantial essays in this collection, Burt Kimmelman suggests that while Heller's poetics has developed 'out of the same poetic traditions' honoured by some of his contemporaries 'who for their own good reasons have sought to dismantle lyrical expression', he has found a way 'to keep statement itself intact and thereby to achieve eloquence in some traditional sense...'. This shrewd awareness of Heller's lyricism is central to David Herd's contribution to the book in his essay 'Poetry on Abandoned Ground', a study of the 2009 collection *Eschaton*. In reminding us of the fact that Michael Heller closes the collection with a prose account of visiting the site of the attack on the Twin Towers, Herd draws our attention to a 'profoundly measured piece of writing' as the poet catches the sombre gravity of the scene through the objects and images left behind: the 'couple who leapt hand in hand from a high floor', an 'image deemed so awful for American television that it never aired again'.

In an essay from 1997, 'Notes on Lyric Poetry or at the Muse's Tomb', Heller gave an account of how the power of the lyric, rather than centring upon being a *product* of thought or of intention, 'comes as a recognition of a gap or rupture in one's thought and intention'. As a poet Heller concentrates upon the borders of language, the moment of invisibility's emergence into the recognizable. He gives full awareness to the importance of names, proper nouns, which 'according to the ancients, is a border, a place where the finite and infinite touch, where the chaos of the undefined has been gathered into the hard knots of language'. David Herd's essay reminds us of the 'mourning field' which 'has no perimeter'. Or, as Michael Heller puts it:

Sorrow has its own space-time continuum, a yesterday or a last month when the heart was ready for its heaviness.

One for the Books

Danielle Hope
Mrs Uomo's Yearbook
Rockingham Press
80 pages, £9.99.

Reviewed by LEAH FRITZ

Unlike Danielle Hope's four previous collections, *Mrs Uomo's Yearbook* is something of a potpourri, divided into five parts including the modestly titled 'Adaptations' at the end, her translations of two Italian poets, Giovanni Pascoli and Eugenio Montale. Hope has travelled a great deal and spent time in several countries, including Italy. She is also a doctor. Born on a Yorkshire farm, her knowledge of the natural world is intimate. It's not surprising, therefore, that the other sections of this book include one on coastal places, another on trees, one on the vagaries of science, and one on – well – people.

The collection begins with a poem that makes extraordinary humane connections. 'Exodus' equates the heroic deliverance from Dunkirk with the harrowing escapes of refugees from Syria and elsewhere:

Sail 2000 miles, 75 years. Crossing from Tripoli to Lampedusa, four rubber dinghies sink. Parched travellers explain money, not drowning, is the hitch. Eight foot
waves.

Conditions like slave ship Zong. Frail vessels with invisible names ghost the deep. Beyond the Harbour Brasserie a flag flutters on the Kent front. Empty shoes carpet the
sea.

Depth of feeling underlies them all, but few of Hope's poems are so impassioned. Some are simply observant, like 'Brighton', in which Hope sketches the panoply of a happy sea-resort where 'Runners stretch ready for their half-marathon, / shops glisten on the esplanade, language schools // buzz and bulge...' It ends with the confession '...But how glum/ I feel, burgled of my boreal gloom.'

Writing about trees, Hope gives us the poem 'Ancient':

'This is the forest I have not left you –
not the sessile oak, nor hornbeam.
No season of thimbleweed,
lesser celandine, purple orchid.

No bluebells in the old sawpit
nor garlic scented ramson
not cool on a hot day
no woodpecker's drum,...'

She plays with formalism or abandons it entirely. In the end of the 'trees' section, she abandons trees, too – well, almost. 'Do Not Disturb' is deliciously about her dog.

There follows the section 'Ordinary People', about whom nothing, of course, is ordinary. In London's Coram Square, an apparent beggar, though 'He has no box or hat / for coins, his case is closed...', plays Bach's partita in G and Elgar on his cello. Here Hope employs *terza rima* without the *rima*, and she does so, too, in the poem 'Alizon', written 'in memory of Alizon Device who was executed in 1612 at the age of 11'. Another poem, 'Calm Down', somewhat obscure, also uses the three-line form, rhyming now and then as the spirit moves her and the song requires. It works, as does the poem in five-line stanzas for 'Patricia', also in blank verse.

There are extraordinary subjects other than people covered in the section dubbed 'Buses, Bus Stops, Hospitals'. For example, 'Convention' describes a wonky 'brain-computer interface (BCI)', a device Hope is sufficiently familiar with to make light of. And then there is 'Mrs Uomo's Yearbook'. Danielle Hope's unlikely alter ego is teaching monetarism to her cat. Mrs Uomo is as wonky as that computer, bless her.

This is an elegantly accomplished collection... one for the books.

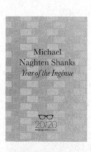

Only

Rupert Brooke, *Sixteen Poems*
Selected by Henry Maas
Greville Press, £7.50

Michael Naghten Shanks,
Year of the Ingénue
Eyewear, £5.00

Stuart Henson, *Feast of Fools*, with illustrations by Bill Sanderson
Shoestring Press, £7.00

Grey Gowrie, *The Right Place*
Greville Press, £4.50

Reviewed by
ALISON BRACKENBURY.

'THINK ONLY THIS OF ME'. Did you grow up knowing only a few poems by Rupert Brooke, including 'The Soldier'? I was startled by much in Henry Maas's new selection. Maas, noting Brooke's 'determination to be modern', concludes that 'Love [...] is his great subject'.

The opening poem, 'The Hill', indeed features boastful lovers:

Proud we were,
And laughed, that had such brave true things to say.
– And then you suddenly cried, and turned away.

After Brooke's characteristic dash, how effectively rhythm (and arrogance) are disrupted. His sonnet flashes through various stanzas: Italianate *abba*, ballad-like *cdcd*. Elsewhere, he creates a 'Sonnet Reversed': anti-climax, via marriage.

Brooke's precocity is not only stylistic. His dancer's rhythms present a lover already dead: 'Most individual and bewildering ghost!—' Exuberant personifications in 'The Funeral of Youth' include 'All, except only *Love. Love* had died long ago'. 'Pain' precedes the stickiness of Grantchester's honey.

This selection would be worth reading for one poem alone: the extraordinary 'Dining-Room Tea', with its vision of time standing still:

the tea,
Hung on the air, an amber stream [...]

The poem is perfectly constructed, its opening finally repeated: 'When you were there, and you, and you'. Brooke's words reach out, past lost coteries, to readers a century later. What might 'The Soldier' have written in 1919? I will only say that it is rare to have the chance to review early harsh judgements. I am grateful for this revealing selection of Brooke's work.

YEAR OF THE INGÉNUE is the excellent debut pamphlet of Michael Naghten Shanks, who has only lived a year longer than Brooke. Technology is in the bloodstream of his poems: 'I scroll through her tumblr'. (Tumblr – I had to check – is a form of microblogging.) There are references to drugs, to film-making: 'centre-screen'. But there are also 'fresh strawberries', and a nightmare sense of a threatening, threatened, physical world: 'you'll hear the glacier crack / and know it's too late to turn and run back'.

Naghten Shanks's poems have a contemporary, 'twitchy' skin, with jump-cut line-endings: 'before you know it, the girl will be / everywhere'. But this collection has good bones. Each section belongs to a season, most featuring the 'Ingénue'. She matures, past her 'fresh' and 'retro' periods, into 'learning to succeed / by perfecting the art of playing herself'. Where Brookes puts wild dashes, Naghten Shanks sets reflective space.

'Love is the subject', suggests S. J. Fowler on this pamphlet's cover. The collection's love story – 'S & I' – only emerges slowly, into clear last lines: 'I started to think about you'; 'would you prefer to be back home on your bed emailing me?' The last of these deeply engaging poems remains enigmatic, with S posed 'for cinematic romance with no sequel'. But first, via Tumblr:

on my phone, on a certain Monday, there exists a picture of you in a blue dress, still.

This is hauntingly lovely, especially the closing line, with its final, rapt, three stresses, a timeless focus for poem and reader.

THERE WAS A TIME WHEN only two words greeted a poet hoping for illustrations: 'Too expensive!' But in Stuart Henson's fine *Feast of Fools*, each of his fourteen poems, 'inspired by a carving on a misericord', has an inspiring partner: a 'scraperboard image' by Bill Sanderson. These illustrations, roughly grained as wood, are riveting. They show a unicorn, a jagged blade inches from its neck; a demon staring delightedly at smartphones... I would only lend this pamphlet to the most trustworthy friend.

Henson's words have a powerfully widening focus, as in 'Dice Players':
through the gut of the fen-country

at the foot of the year's dark cross
they've already lost
in life's lottery

His rhymes are often delayed, only chiming after a couple of stanzas. They build up subtly but authoritatively, just as the carvings illustrate a moral. But his endings are pithy, as in 'Vanitas': 'the mirror has two other masters: / time and truth'. The poems are not only bound to the misericord's century. Dentistry may be 'blood-floored and vicious', but Henson's gossips tap MacBooks.

Only poetry's speech can grow as charged as Henson's words to a girl who entraps a unicorn: 'yes / what you'd betrayed was love'. His pamphlet ends with one of the strangest of medieval images: the Green Man. Meaning leaps across space, between two worlds:

so I utter
leaves

Strength, like a young oak leaf's, is matched by the delicacy of lightly-run syllables: only 'one cell / at the tongue-tip of being.' 'Only connect', wrote E. M. Forster. It is rarely done with such grace.

GREY GOWRIE'S *THE RIGHT PLACE* is a tiny chapbook, which I enjoyed immensely. Sub-titled 'A Neo-Classical Primer', it contains only sixteen short poems. I am wary of poems which feed parasitically upon other poets' words, but robust replies are another matter.

Fifteen of these poems include a quotation. (Its author is often named only in a footnote.) Each is a trigger for rueful reflection, sharp riposte – or literary advice: 'Fatal to start a stanza with the weather.' Rhymes are recklessly effective. Metres are exuberant rather than precise. No Tumblr here! 'Do not Text or Tweet it. Write a letter.'

Gowrie, born in 1939, does not share Brooke's youthful enthusiasm for death. I can only quote his final poem in full: a dramatised reaction to a line by Shelley, which should be better-known.

I met Murder on the way.
He raised his hat and said, 'Good day.'
I hurried on, I knew he lied,
And tipped my own, to Suicide.

Readers may be shocked that, elsewhere, Gowrie rhymes Plath's 'black shoe' with 'Jimmy Choo'. But jokes can boomerang. The humour may prove more damning to Choo-buyers.

Poems should only have one review. But, with apologies to readers, subjects, and editors, here is my second review of the infectious lines in 'The Right Place'. These may not be the right words. But for once, and once only, they rhyme:

Grey Gowrie plucks quotes from the great.
His pen is sharp and Latinate.
Though he says 'Rot', he hits the mark.
This book steps lightly into dark.

Sam Adams edited *Poetry Wales* in the early 1970s and has been a contributor to PN Review since 1982. **Michael Alexander**'s verse translations of Old English poetry are published by Penguin Classics and Anvil. More recently he has published *A History of English Literature, Medievalism: The Middle Ages in Modern England*, and *Reading Shakespeare*. **Rowland Bagnall** is a twenty-four-year-old poet from Oxford. His writing has previously appeared in *Poetry London*, *The Quietus*, and *Oxford Poetry* among others. He is working towards a first collection. **Alison Brackenbury**'s ninth collection of poems, *Skies*, was published by Carcanet in February 2016. New poems can be read on her website, alisonbrackenbury.co.uk. **Claire Crowther** has published three collections of poetry. The first, *Stretch of Closures*, was shortlisted for the Aldeburgh Prize. Her current collection is *On Narrowness* (Shearsman). **Vahni Capildeo** is a British Trinidadian writer. *Simple Complex Shapes* (Shearsman, 2015) and *Measures of Expatriation* (Carcanet, 2016) are her most recent books. **Leah Fritz**'s poetry 'is always enjoyable for its intelligence, wit, satirical sting and freshness of wording,' wrote Christopher Middleton. *Whatever Sends the Music into Time: New and Selected Poems* is published by Salmon Poetry, Ireland. **Liam Guilar**'s most recent book is *Rough Spun to Close Weave*. *Anhaga*, an improvisation on 'The Wanderer', will be published in 2016. Details at www.liamguilar.com, arguments at ladygodivaandme.blogspot.com.au. **Adam Heardman** is a poet from Newcastle upon Tyne, studying towards an MSt. in Modern Literature at Oxford. **Henry King** studied at the University of Glasgow and teaches at Malmö University, Sweden. His poems and translations have appeared in *PN Review*, *Stand*, *Modern Poetry in Translation*, and elsewhere. **Thomas Kinsella** resigned from Irish Department of Finance in 1965 for a career in poetry, and now lives in Philadelphia. He was made Freeman of the City of Dublin in 2005. His most recent collection is *Late Poems* (Carcanet, 2013); translations from Irish include the eighth-century prose epic *Táin Bó Cuailgne*. He is Editor, with translations, of the *New Oxford Book of Irish Verse*. **Eric Langley** is a lecturer in Shakespeare at UCL. His book, *Suicide and Narcissism in the Works of Shakespeare*, was published by OUP, and his poetry collection, *Raking Light*, will be published by Carcanet in 2017. **Sue Leigh**'s work has been published in a number of magazines and journals, among them *Oxford Magazine*, *Planet*, the *TLS*

and *The Warwick Review*. Her poems were also included in *Oxford Poets 2007: An Anthology*. She won the BBC Proms Poetry Competition in 2014 and was shortlisted for the Bridport Prize in 2015. **Owen Lowery**'s poetry has appeared in *Stand*, *PN Review*, and *The Observer*. His two poetry collections, *Otherwise Unchanged* and *Rego Retold*, were published by Carcanet in 2012 and 2015. **Carol Mavor**'s *Aurelia: Art and Literature Through the Eyes and Mouth of the Fairy Tale* is forthcoming from Reaktion (2017). Currently, she is writing a novel entitled *Like a Lake: An Elegy of Love with Pictures*. **Sinéad Morrissey** is the author of five collections, the most recent of which, *Parallax* (2013), won the T. S. Eliot Prize and the Irish Times Poetry Award. She lectures in Creative Writing at the Seamus Heaney Centre for Poetry in Belfast. **Andrew Wynn Owen** is an Examination Fellow at All Souls College, Oxford. He received an Eric Gregory Award in 2015 and Oxford University's Newdigate Prize in 2014. **Ian Pople**'s *Saving Spaces* is published by Arc. **Sheenagh Pugh** lived most of her life in Wales but now lives in Shetland. Her latest collection is *Short Days, Long Shadows* (Seren, 2014). **Sam Quill** lives in south London. The Fourteen Sonnets are his first poems in print. **Amali Rodrigo**'s first collection *Lotus Gatherers* is published by Bloodaxe in May 2016. She is a PhD candidate and Associate Lecturer at Lancaster University. She lives in London. **C.K. Stead**'s new collection of reviews, lectures, interviews and literary journalism, *Shelf Life*, will be published by Auckland University Press in June. He is New Zealand Poet Laureate for 2015–2017. **Colin Still** is a film-maker who makes documentaries on poetry & contemporary music. He is currently working on films on Robert Creeley and Jerome Rothenberg; he is also editing an anthology for Carcanet on the Black Mountain poets. **Nicolas Tredell** has contributed to *PN Review* for thirty-five years. A new edition of *Conversations with Critics*, consisting of interviews conducted for *PNR* between 1990 and 2003, has recently appeared. **Rory Waterman**'s *Tonight the Summer's Over* (2013) was a PBS Recommendation, shortlisted for the Heaney Prize. He teaches at NTU, co-edits *New Walk*, and writes for the *TLS* and other publications. **Patrick Worsnip** read Classics and Modern Languages at Merton College, Oxford. From 1971 to 2012 he worked as a correspondent for Reuters. He is currently working on a new translation of the poems of Propertius.

Editors
Michael Schmidt (General)
Luke Allan (Deputy)

Cover
Hannah Devereux
2016

Type
Set in Arnhem Pro and Averta
by LA.

Editorial address
The Editors at the address on
the right. Manuscripts cannot be
returned unless accompanied by a
stamped self-addressed envelope
or international reply coupon.

Subscriptions (6 issues)
individuals: £39/$86
institutions: £49/$105
to: PN Review, Alliance House
30 Cross Street, Manchester
M2 7AQ, UK

Represented by
Compass Independent Publishing
  Services Ltd
Great West House, Great West Road
Brentford TW8 9DF, UK
sales@compass-ips.london

Trade distributors
NBN International
10 Thornbury Road
Plymouth PL6 7PP, UK
orders@nbninternational.com

Copyright
© 2016 Poetry Nation Review
All rights reserved
ISBN 978-1-78410-140-4
ISSN 0144-7076

Supported by